Bank Statement Mortgage Loan Refinancing & Cash-Out Strategies

How to Refinance and Access Equity Without Using Tax Returns

By Joseph G. Correa

Licensed Mortgage Broker

Finibi Mortgage

Copyright & Legal Notice

Published by Live Stronger Faster

The information provided in this book is for educational and informational purposes only and does not constitute financial, legal, tax, or investment advice. Although the author is a licensed mortgage professional, the content presented is general in nature and is not intended as personalized guidance for any specific individual or financial situation.

The strategies, structuring methods, and examples discussed in this book are illustrative and educational in nature. They are intended to demonstrate concepts related to bank statement mortgage loan qualification and structuring, including deposit analysis, expense ratio application, and investor guideline interpretation. These examples do not represent guaranteed outcomes or approvals. Results may vary significantly based on individual financial profiles, documentation, credit history, property type, and lender-specific requirements.

The author and publisher make no representations or warranties regarding the accuracy, completeness, or applicability of the content and disclaim any liability for errors, omissions, or outcomes resulting from the use or misuse of the information contained in this book.

First Edition, 2026

Table of Contents

Introduction

In the journey of building wealth through real estate, few strategies are as powerful—and as misunderstood—as refinancing and accessing equity. For self-employed borrowers, entrepreneurs, and business owners, the challenge has never been a lack of income or opportunity. The challenge has always been documentation. Traditional mortgage guidelines rely heavily on tax returns, often penalizing those who take full advantage of legal deductions, reinvest in their businesses, or operate with fluctuating income streams. As a result, many highly successful individuals appear underqualified on paper, despite having strong cash flow and substantial assets. This is where bank statement mortgage loan refinancing and cash-out strategies step in as a transformative solution.

This book is designed to open the door to a new level of financial control and opportunity. It is not just about refinancing a property; it is about unlocking the hidden potential within your existing real estate portfolio. Whether you own a primary residence, an investment property, or a portfolio of income-producing assets, the equity you have built over time represents stored wealth. The key is knowing how to access that wealth strategically, efficiently, and without triggering unnecessary obstacles through traditional documentation methods. By using bank statement income instead of tax returns, borrowers gain the ability to present their true financial strength and qualify for refinancing solutions that align with their real-world cash flow.

Refinancing is often misunderstood as simply lowering an interest rate or changing loan terms. While those are certainly benefits, the true power of refinancing lies in its ability to reposition your financial foundation. A well-structured refinance can reduce monthly obligations, improve cash flow, eliminate high-interest debt, and provide liquidity for new investments. When combined with a cash-out strategy, refinancing becomes a wealth-building engine. It allows you to convert equity into usable capital—capital that can be reinvested into additional properties, business ventures, or other income-generating opportunities. For the self-employed borrower, this approach can be the difference between being financially stuck and achieving exponential growth.

Bank statement mortgage loan refinancing takes this concept even further by removing one of the biggest barriers to entry: tax return limitations. Instead of relying on net income after deductions, lenders evaluate deposits and cash flow patterns within your personal or business bank statements. This provides a more accurate representation of your earning ability and financial stability. It also allows borrowers who may have written off significant expenses—or who operate in industries with complex financial structures—to qualify based on what they actually earn, not what is reflected on a tax document. This shift in perspective is critical, and understanding how to leverage it properly is one of the primary goals of this book.

As you move through this material, you will begin to see that not all refinancing strategies are created equal. There are multiple approaches to structuring a bank statement refinance, and each one depends on your specific goals. Some borrowers aim to reduce their interest rate and monthly payment. Others are focused on extracting equity to consolidate debt or fund new investments. Still others are looking to transition from one loan type to another, improve terms, or reposition their portfolio for long-term growth. The ability to match the right strategy to the right scenario is what separates a basic refinance from a powerful financial move.

Cash-out refinancing, in particular, is one of the most impactful tools available to real estate investors and homeowners alike. By tapping into the equity you have built, you can create liquidity without selling your property. This means you continue to benefit from appreciation, rental income, and tax advantages while simultaneously accessing capital. For investors, this can be used to acquire additional properties, scale a portfolio, or improve existing assets. For homeowners, it can provide the funds needed for renovations, debt consolidation, or major life investments. The flexibility of this strategy is what makes it so valuable, but it also requires careful planning and execution to ensure long-term success.

Debt consolidation is another powerful application of bank statement refinancing. Many borrowers carry high-interest credit card debt, personal loans, or other obligations that drain their monthly cash flow. By consolidating these debts into a mortgage with a lower interest rate, borrowers can significantly reduce their monthly payments and improve their overall financial stability. This not only frees up cash flow but also strengthens the borrower's profile for future financing opportunities. When structured correctly, a debt consolidation refinance can serve as a reset button—providing clarity, control, and a path forward.

Liquidity strategies go beyond simply accessing cash; they involve using that cash strategically to create more income, reduce risk, or position yourself for future opportunities. For example, pulling equity from one property to fund the down payment on another can accelerate portfolio growth. Using cash-out funds to improve a property can increase its value and rental income potential. Allocating capital into business expansion can generate additional revenue streams that further strengthen your financial profile. The key is understanding how to deploy capital effectively, and this book will guide you through that process step by step.

Another important aspect of bank statement refinancing is understanding lender guidelines and how they differ from traditional loans. While these programs offer greater flexibility, they also require a strategic approach to documentation and presentation. Lenders will analyze bank statements for consistency, stability, and patterns. They will evaluate deposit sources, expense ratios, and overall cash flow trends. Borrowers who understand how to present clean, organized financials—and who know how to structure their accounts in advance—will have a significant advantage. Throughout this book, you will learn how to position yourself for success by aligning your financial profile with lender expectations.

It is also important to recognize the role of timing in refinancing decisions. Market conditions, interest rates, property values, and personal financial goals all play a role in determining the right moment to refinance. Acting too early or too late can impact the effectiveness of your strategy. By understanding how to evaluate these factors, you can make informed decisions that maximize your benefits and minimize risk. This book will provide you with the tools to assess your situation and determine the optimal timing for your refinance. For borrowers with complex financial situations, bank statement refinancing offers a level of adaptability that traditional loans simply cannot match. Whether you have multiple income streams, seasonal earnings, or unconventional business structures, these programs can be tailored to fit your needs. The key is knowing how to navigate the process, communicate your financial story, and work with lenders who understand the nuances of self-employed income. This book is designed to give you that knowledge and confidence.

As you continue reading, you will gain a deeper understanding of how to structure cash-out transactions, evaluate loan-to-value limits, manage reserves, and balance risk with opportunity. You will learn how to analyze your own financial profile, identify strengths and weaknesses, and make adjustments that improve your chances of approval. You will also discover how to think like a lender—anticipating questions, addressing concerns, and presenting a clear, compelling case for your loan.

Ultimately, this book is about empowerment. It is about giving you the ability to take control of your financial future by leveraging the assets you already have. It is about breaking free from the limitations of traditional underwriting and embracing a more accurate, flexible approach to qualifying for a mortgage. And most importantly, it is about showing you how to turn equity into opportunity—how to transform what you have built into a foundation for even greater success. The strategies outlined in this book are not theoretical. They are practical, actionable, and designed to be implemented in real-world scenarios. Whether you are refinancing your first property or optimizing a large portfolio, the principles you will learn here can be applied immediately. By the time you finish this book, you will not only understand how bank statement mortgage loan refinancing works—you will know how to use it as a powerful tool to build wealth, increase cash flow, and achieve long-term financial independence.

Welcome to the next level of mortgage strategy.

Chapter 1

Understanding Bank Statement Refinancing and Cash-Out Fundamentals

Refinancing is one of the most powerful financial tools available to homeowners and real estate investors, yet it is often misunderstood or underutilized—especially among self-employed individuals. At its core, refinancing is the process of replacing an existing mortgage with a new one, typically with different terms, a new interest rate, or a different loan structure. For many borrowers, the goal is simple: reduce monthly payments or secure a better rate. However, in the world of bank statement mortgage loans, refinancing takes on a much deeper and more strategic role. It becomes a tool not just for saving money, but for unlocking equity, restructuring debt, and creating new financial opportunities without relying on traditional tax return documentation.

Bank statement refinancing is specifically designed for borrowers whose true income is not accurately reflected on their tax returns. This includes business owners, freelancers, consultants, and entrepreneurs who often write off significant expenses to reduce taxable income. While this strategy may be beneficial from a tax perspective, it can create challenges when applying for traditional mortgage loans, which rely heavily on net income after deductions. Bank statement loans solve this problem by focusing on actual cash flow—what is coming into the borrower's accounts—rather than what is reported on tax documents. This allows lenders to evaluate the borrower's real earning power and approve loans based on a more accurate financial picture.

When applying for a bank statement refinance, lenders typically review 12 or 24 months of personal or business bank statements. They analyze deposits to determine qualifying income, often applying an expense factor if business statements are used. This expense factor represents estimated business expenses and can vary depending on the borrower's industry or whether a CPA provides a profit and loss statement. For personal bank statements, lenders may use 100% of eligible deposits as income, while business accounts may be adjusted by an expense ratio—commonly ranging from 10% to 50%. Understanding how these calculations work is critical, as they directly impact how much a borrower can qualify for when refinancing.

One of the most important distinctions in refinancing is the difference between a rate-and-term refinance and a cash-out refinance. A rate-and-term refinance focuses on improving the loan's terms—such as lowering the interest rate, changing the loan duration, or switching from an adjustable-rate mortgage to a fixed-rate mortgage—without significantly increasing the loan balance. In contrast, a cash-out refinance allows the borrower to access a portion of their home's equity by replacing the existing loan with a larger one and receiving the difference in cash. This cash can then be used for a variety of purposes, including debt consolidation, property improvements, or investing in additional real estate.

Equity plays a central role in any refinancing strategy. Equity is the difference between the current market value of a property and the outstanding mortgage balance. As property values increase and loan balances decrease over time, equity builds. This equity represents a form of stored wealth that can be accessed through refinancing. However, lenders impose limits on how much equity can be withdrawn, typically expressed as a maximum loan-to-value (LTV) ratio. For example, if a lender allows up to 80% LTV on a cash-out refinance, and a property is worth $500,000, the maximum loan amount would be $400,000. If the current loan balance is $250,000, the borrower could potentially access up to $150,000 in cash, minus closing costs and fees.

In bank statement refinancing, LTV limits may vary depending on factors such as credit score, property type, and loan size.

Borrowers with strong credit profiles and significant reserves may qualify for higher LTVs, while those with lower credit scores may face more conservative limits. This is where compensating factors come into play. Compensating factors include elements such as high cash reserves, low debt-to-income ratios, strong income consistency, or significant equity in other properties. These factors can help offset perceived risks and improve the borrower's chances of approval.

Another key concept in bank statement refinancing is the importance of clean and consistent financial documentation. Lenders are not just looking at how much money is deposited into an account—they are also analyzing patterns, consistency, and sources of income. Large, irregular deposits without clear documentation may raise red flags, while consistent monthly deposits from identifiable sources strengthen the borrower's profile. Borrowers who understand this process can take proactive steps to organize their finances, separate personal and business accounts, and maintain clear records that support their income claims.

Timing is also a critical factor in refinancing decisions. Interest rates fluctuate based on market conditions, and even small changes in rates can significantly impact monthly payments and overall loan costs. Additionally, property values may rise or fall over time, affecting the amount of equity available. Borrowers must consider these factors when deciding when to refinance. Acting at the right time can maximize benefits, while poor timing can limit opportunities or reduce potential gains.

For many borrowers, refinancing is not a one-time event but part of a larger financial strategy. Real estate investors, in particular, often use refinancing as a way to recycle capital. By purchasing a property, increasing its value, and then refinancing to pull out equity, investors can reinvest that capital into additional properties. This process, sometimes referred to as the BRRRR strategy (Buy, Rehab, Rent, Refinance, Repeat), allows investors to scale their portfolios more rapidly. Bank statement loans play a crucial role in this strategy, as they provide flexible qualification options for borrowers with non-traditional income.

Debt consolidation is another powerful application of refinancing. High-interest debts such as credit cards and personal loans can significantly impact cash flow and financial stability. By consolidating these debts into a mortgage with a lower interest rate, borrowers can reduce their monthly obligations and simplify their finances. This not only improves cash flow but can also enhance credit profiles over time, creating additional opportunities for future financing.

Ultimately, understanding the fundamentals of bank statement refinancing and cash-out strategies is the foundation for making informed financial decisions. It is about more than just securing a loan—it is about leveraging your assets, optimizing your financial structure, and creating opportunities for growth. As you move forward, you will build on these concepts and learn how to apply them in real-world scenarios, allowing you to take full advantage of the flexibility and power that bank statement mortgage loans provide.

Real-Life Math Example: Applying Bank Statement Cash-Out Refinancing Strategy

Consider a self-employed borrower named David, who owns a primary residence valued at $600,000. David originally purchased the home several years ago and currently has an outstanding mortgage balance of $320,000 with an interest rate of 5.75%. Over time, the property has appreciated in value, and David has built substantial equity. However, due to aggressive tax write-offs related to his business, his reported income on tax returns appears relatively low, making it difficult for him to qualify for a traditional refinance. Instead, David explores a bank statement refinance to access his equity and improve his financial situation.

David provides 12 months of personal bank statements showing consistent deposits averaging $18,000 per month.

Since these are personal statements, the lender uses 100% of eligible deposits to calculate qualifying income. This results in a monthly qualifying income of $18,000. Based on lender guidelines, David is approved for a new loan with a maximum debt-to-income ratio that supports a higher loan amount than his current balance.

The lender allows a maximum loan-to-value ratio of 80% for a cash-out refinance. With a property value of $600,000, the maximum loan amount David can obtain is $480,000. After paying off his existing mortgage balance of $320,000, this leaves $160,000 available. From this amount, closing costs and fees—estimated at $10,000—are deducted, resulting in net cash-out proceeds of $150,000.

David decides to allocate this $150,000 strategically. He uses $50,000 to pay off high-interest credit card debt that was costing him approximately $1,200 per month in payments. By eliminating this debt, he immediately improves his monthly cash flow. He then invests $70,000 as a down payment on a rental property, leveraging financing to acquire an asset that generates $2,000 per month in rental income. The remaining $30,000 is set aside as reserves, strengthening his financial profile and providing a safety net.

The new mortgage is structured at a 6.25% interest rate with a loan amount of $480,000. While the rate is slightly higher than traditional loans, the overall financial impact is positive. David's previous mortgage payment was approximately $1,860 per month. The new payment increases to around $2,950 per month. However, after eliminating $1,200 in credit card payments and adding $2,000 in rental income, David's net monthly cash flow improves significantly.

Before refinancing, David's total monthly obligations were approximately $3,060 ($1,860 mortgage + $1,200 credit cards). After refinancing, his obligations increase to $2,950 for the mortgage, but his credit card payments are eliminated. Additionally, his rental income offsets the new payment. When factoring in the rental income, David effectively reduces his net housing cost while building long-term wealth through real estate.

Over time, the benefits compound. The rental property appreciates in value, generates consistent income, and provides tax advantages. Meanwhile, David's improved cash flow allows him to reinvest in his business and pursue additional opportunities. The $150,000 in equity that was once locked in his home is now actively working to generate returns and improve his financial position.

This example illustrates the power of bank statement cash-out refinancing when applied strategically. It is not just about accessing equity—it is about using that equity to create leverage, increase income, and build a stronger financial foundation. By understanding the numbers, structuring the loan correctly, and deploying capital effectively, borrowers can transform a simple refinance into a powerful wealth-building strategy.

Chapter 2

Cash-Out Refinance Strategies for Wealth Building and Financial Control

Cash-out refinancing is one of the most powerful strategies available to homeowners and real estate investors, yet it is often approached without a clear plan or long-term vision. When used correctly—especially within the framework of bank statement mortgage loans—it becomes a strategic financial tool capable of transforming equity into income, opportunity, and long-term wealth. For self-employed borrowers and entrepreneurs, this strategy is particularly valuable because it allows them to access capital without relying on traditional income documentation, which often fails to capture the full scope of their earning potential. In this chapter, we will explore how to use cash-out refinancing not just as a transaction, but as a deliberate and calculated wealth-building strategy.

At its foundation, a cash-out refinance replaces your existing mortgage with a new, larger loan, allowing you to extract a portion of your home's equity in cash. This concept is simple, but the execution is where strategy comes into play. Every dollar pulled out of a property should have a purpose. Without a plan, cash-out refinancing can lead to increased debt without meaningful returns. With a plan, it becomes a tool for leverage—turning idle equity into active capital that generates income, reduces liabilities, or creates new opportunities.

One of the most effective ways to use cash-out refinancing is for real estate portfolio expansion. Investors often find themselves equity-rich but cash-poor, with significant value tied up in properties but limited liquidity to acquire new assets. A cash-out refinance solves this problem by converting equity into usable funds that can be deployed as down payments on additional properties. This creates a cycle of growth where one property leads to another, and another, allowing investors to scale their portfolios without waiting years to accumulate savings. When combined with bank statement loan qualification, this strategy becomes even more accessible for self-employed investors who may not qualify under traditional guidelines.

Another strategic use of cash-out refinancing is property improvement and forced appreciation. By reinvesting extracted equity into renovations or upgrades, borrowers can increase the value of their property, which in turn creates additional equity. This is particularly powerful in investment properties, where improvements can also lead to higher rental income. For example, upgrading kitchens, bathrooms, or adding amenities can significantly increase both property value and cash flow. This creates a compounding effect: higher property value leads to more equity, which can be accessed again in the future, continuing the cycle of growth.

Debt consolidation remains one of the most immediate and impactful uses of cash-out refinancing. High-interest debt—such as credit cards, personal loans, or business obligations—can significantly drain monthly cash flow and limit financial flexibility. By consolidating these debts into a mortgage with a lower interest rate, borrowers can reduce their overall monthly payments and simplify their financial obligations. For self-employed individuals, this can be especially beneficial, as it stabilizes cash flow and improves their ability to reinvest in their business or pursue new opportunities. The key is to ensure that the debt being consolidated is not recreated after the refinance, as that would undermine the long-term benefits of the strategy.

Liquidity is another critical component of financial success, and cash-out refinancing provides a way to build and maintain it. Having access to cash reserves allows borrowers to respond quickly to opportunities, handle unexpected expenses, and navigate market fluctuations with confidence. In real estate investing, liquidity can mean the difference between securing a great deal and missing out. By maintaining a portion of cash-out funds as reserves, borrowers strengthen their financial position and create a buffer that reduces risk. This is particularly important in uncertain market conditions, where flexibility and preparedness are essential.

A more advanced strategy involves using cash-out refinancing to reposition an entire financial portfolio. This may include paying off underperforming assets, reallocating capital into higher-yield investments, or restructuring debt to improve overall efficiency. For example, a borrower may choose to sell or refinance a low-performing property and use the proceeds to acquire a higher-income asset. Alternatively, they may use cash-out funds to invest in a business venture that generates higher returns than the cost of borrowing. This type of strategic thinking requires a clear understanding of both short-term and long-term goals, as well as the discipline to execute a well-defined plan.

Risk management is an essential consideration in any cash-out refinance strategy. While accessing equity can create opportunities, it also increases leverage, which can amplify both gains and losses. Borrowers must carefully evaluate their ability to manage higher loan balances and ensure that their income—whether from employment, business, or investments—is sufficient to support the new obligations. Maintaining adequate reserves, diversifying income sources, and avoiding over-leveraging are key principles that help mitigate risk and ensure long-term success. Another important factor is understanding the cost of capital. While mortgage interest rates are generally lower than other forms of debt, they still represent a cost that must be justified by the returns generated from the use of funds. Borrowers should evaluate whether the expected return on investment exceeds the cost of borrowing. For example, if a cash-out refinance results in a 6.5% interest rate, the funds should ideally be used in a way that generates a return higher than 6.5%. This ensures that the strategy creates positive financial leverage rather than eroding wealth over time.

Bank statement loans add another layer of flexibility to these strategies by allowing borrowers to qualify based on actual cash flow rather than tax returns. This is particularly beneficial for entrepreneurs who reinvest heavily in their businesses or who have variable income. By presenting consistent and well-documented bank statements, borrowers can demonstrate their true earning capacity and access financing that aligns with their financial reality. This flexibility opens the door to more aggressive and creative strategies that may not be possible under traditional lending guidelines.

Timing and market conditions also play a critical role in the success of cash-out refinancing. Interest rates, property values, and economic trends all influence the effectiveness of a refinance. Borrowers should monitor these factors and be prepared to act when conditions are favorable. For example, rising property values can increase available equity, while stable or declining interest rates can improve loan terms. Understanding how to read and respond to these conditions is an essential skill for anyone looking to maximize the benefits of refinancing.

Ultimately, cash-out refinancing is not just about accessing money—it is about creating a system for growth, stability, and financial independence. It requires a shift in mindset from viewing a home as simply a place to live, to seeing it as a financial asset that can be leveraged strategically. By combining this mindset with the flexibility of bank statement mortgage loans, borrowers gain the ability to take control of their financial future in ways that were previously out of reach.

Real-Life Math Example: Scaling Wealth Through Strategic Cash-Out Refinancing

Let's talk about a borrower named Maria, a self-employed consultant who owns a primary residence and one investment property. Her primary residence is valued at $700,000 with a current mortgage balance of $350,000. Her investment property is valued at $400,000 with a mortgage balance of $220,000. Maria has built significant equity in both properties but lacks the liquidity needed to expand her real estate portfolio. Because her tax returns show reduced income due to business deductions, she chooses to pursue a bank statement cash-out refinance.

Maria provides 24 months of bank statements showing consistent deposits averaging $22,000 per month. The lender uses this to calculate her qualifying income. Based on her financial profile, she is approved for a cash-out refinance on her primary residence with a maximum loan-to-value ratio of 75%. This allows for a new loan amount of $525,000 on her primary residence ($700,000 × 75%). After paying off her existing mortgage of $350,000, she has $175,000 in available equity. After closing costs of $12,000, Maria receives approximately $163,000 in cash.

Maria develops a strategic plan for this capital. She allocates $100,000 as down payments on two additional investment properties, each priced at $250,000. With 20% down on each property ($50,000 per property), she secures financing for both. Each property generates $1,800 per month in rental income, resulting in a combined monthly income of $3,600. The mortgage payments on these properties total $2,400 per month, leaving a net cash flow of $1,200.

She uses $40,000 of the remaining funds to renovate her existing investment property, increasing its value from

$400,000 to $460,000 and raising rental income from $2,000 to $2,600 per month. This adds an additional $600 in monthly cash flow. The final $23,000 is kept as reserves, strengthening her financial position and ensuring she meets lender requirements for future financing.

Maria's new mortgage on her primary residence is $525,000 at a 6.75% interest rate, resulting in a monthly payment of approximately $3,400. Previously, her payment was $2,100. While her mortgage payment increased by $1,300, her rental income increased significantly. Before refinancing, her total rental income was $2,000 per month. After implementing her strategy, her total rental income is now $6,200 per month ($2,600 from the renovated property plus $3,600 from the two new properties).

When comparing the numbers, Maria's financial position has improved dramatically. Her additional rental income of $4,200 per month ($6,200 new total minus $2,000 original) more than offsets the $1,300 increase in her primary mortgage payment. This results in a net positive cash flow increase of $2,900 per month. Additionally, her total real estate portfolio value has grown from $1.1 million ($700,000 + $400,000) to $1.66 million ($700,000 + $460,000 + $500,000 from two new properties).

Over time, Maria benefits from property appreciation, rental income, and tax advantages. Assuming a conservative annual appreciation rate of 4%, her portfolio could increase in value by over $66,000 per year. Combined with her increased cash flow, this creates a powerful wealth-building engine. The initial $163,000 extracted from her primary residence has been transformed into multiple income-producing assets, demonstrating the power of strategic cash-out refinancing.

This example highlights how a well-planned cash-out refinance can go far beyond simply accessing equity. It can serve as the foundation for scaling a real estate portfolio, increasing cash flow, and building long-term wealth. By understanding the numbers, aligning them with clear goals, and executing a strategic plan, borrowers can turn their existing assets into a platform for financial growth and independence.

Chapter 3

Debt Consolidation and Cash Flow Optimization Using Bank Statement Refinancing

One of the most immediate and life-changing applications of a bank statement cash-out refinance is debt consolidation and cash flow optimization. While many borrowers initially approach refinancing with the goal of accessing equity or investing in additional properties, the reality is that a strong financial foundation begins with controlling and optimizing cash flow. For self-employed borrowers, entrepreneurs, and investors, inconsistent income and high-interest obligations can create pressure that limits growth. Debt consolidation through a bank statement refinance provides a strategic way to simplify finances, reduce monthly obligations, and regain control over cash flow—without relying on traditional income documentation.

Debt, in itself, is not inherently negative. In fact, when used strategically, debt can be a powerful tool for leverage and growth. However, not all debt is created equal. High-interest consumer debt—such as credit cards, personal loans, and unsecured lines of credit—can quickly become a financial burden. These types of debts often carry interest rates ranging from 15% to 30% or more, making them significantly more expensive than mortgage debt. When a borrower carries multiple high-interest obligations, a large portion of their monthly income is consumed by interest payments rather than building wealth. This is where the concept of debt consolidation becomes essential.

A bank statement refinance allows borrowers to convert high-interest, short-term debt into lower-interest, long-term mortgage debt. By doing so, borrowers can significantly reduce their monthly payments and improve their overall financial efficiency. Instead of juggling multiple payments with varying due dates and interest rates, they can consolidate everything into a single, predictable mortgage payment. This simplification not only reduces financial stress but also improves budgeting and long-term planning.

For self-employed borrowers, this strategy is particularly powerful because it aligns with how lenders evaluate risk. High monthly debt obligations can negatively impact a borrower's debt-to-income ratio, making it more difficult to qualify for future financing. By consolidating debt into a mortgage, borrowers can lower their monthly obligations relative to their income, improving their qualification profile. When combined with bank statement income calculations, this creates a pathway for borrowers to access better financing options in the future.

Cash flow optimization goes beyond simply reducing payments—it is about creating a financial structure that supports growth and flexibility. When monthly obligations are reduced, borrowers free up capital that can be redirected toward investments, business expansion, or savings. This creates a compounding effect where improved cash flow leads to more opportunities, which in turn generate additional income. Over time, this cycle can significantly accelerate wealth building.

One of the key principles of successful debt consolidation is intentionality. Borrowers must have a clear plan for how they will use the savings generated from lower payments. Without discipline, there is a risk of accumulating new debt after consolidation, which can lead to an even worse financial position. The goal is not just to move debt around, but to eliminate high-cost obligations and create a more efficient financial structure. This requires a commitment to financial discipline and a focus on long-term goals.

Another important consideration is the cost of extending debt over a longer period. While mortgage interest rates are typically lower than consumer debt rates, mortgages are amortized over longer terms, such as 30 years. This means that while monthly payments may decrease, the total interest paid over time could increase if the borrower does not take additional steps to manage the loan. Strategies such as making extra principal payments, refinancing again in the future, or using improved cash flow to invest in higher-return opportunities can help offset this effect.

Bank statement refinancing introduces an additional layer of flexibility by allowing borrowers to qualify based on their actual cash flow rather than their tax returns. This is especially beneficial for those who have taken significant deductions or whose income varies from year to year. By presenting consistent bank deposits, borrowers can demonstrate their ability to support the new loan structure, even if their tax returns suggest otherwise. This opens the door to debt consolidation strategies that may not be available through traditional lending channels.

Credit profile improvement is another major benefit of debt consolidation. High credit card balances and multiple open accounts can negatively impact a borrower's credit score. By paying off these balances through a cash-out refinance, borrowers can reduce their credit utilization ratio, which is a key factor in credit scoring models. Over time, this can lead to improved credit scores, better loan terms, and increased access to financing options. For borrowers with lower credit scores, this can be a critical step in rebuilding their financial profile.

Liquidity also plays a role in debt consolidation strategies. While it may be tempting to use all available cash-out funds to pay off debt, maintaining a portion of those funds as reserves is essential. Reserves provide a safety net for unexpected expenses and help ensure that borrowers do not need to rely on high-interest debt again in the future. Lenders also view reserves as a positive compensating factor, which can improve loan approval chances and terms.

Timing is another factor that influences the effectiveness of debt consolidation through refinancing. Interest rates, property values, and the borrower's financial situation all play a role in determining the optimal time to refinance. For example, rising property values can increase available equity, making it easier to consolidate larger amounts of debt. Similarly, favorable interest rates can enhance the benefits of consolidation by reducing the cost of borrowing. Borrowers should evaluate these factors carefully and consider both current and future financial conditions when making their decision.

For real estate investors, debt consolidation can also be used as a tool to improve portfolio performance. By reducing personal financial obligations, investors can free up capital to reinvest in their properties or acquire new assets. This creates a more efficient allocation of resources and supports long-term growth. Additionally, improved cash flow can make it easier to qualify for additional loans, further expanding investment opportunities.

Ultimately, debt consolidation through bank statement refinancing is about creating a more efficient and sustainable financial structure. It is about reducing unnecessary costs, improving cash flow, and positioning yourself for future growth. When executed correctly, it can provide immediate relief while also setting the stage for long-term financial success. As you continue through this book, you will learn how to integrate this strategy with other refinancing techniques to create a comprehensive approach to wealth building.

Real-Life Math Example: Transforming Financial Stability Through Debt Consolidation

Consider a borrower named Alex, a self-employed business owner with a strong income but a complex financial situation. Alex owns a primary residence valued at $650,000 with a current mortgage balance of $300,000 at an interest rate of 5.5%, resulting in a monthly payment of approximately

$1,700. In addition to his mortgage, Alex carries several high-interest debts: $40,000 in credit card debt at an average interest rate of 22% with monthly payments of $1,200, a $25,000 personal loan at 14% with a monthly payment of $580, and a $15,000 business line of credit at 12% with a monthly payment of $400. In total, Alex's monthly debt obligations are $3,880.

Despite earning an average of $20,000 per month based on bank statement deposits, Alex feels financially constrained due to his high monthly obligations. His tax returns show significantly lower income due to business deductions, making it difficult for him to qualify for a traditional refinance. He decides to pursue a bank statement cash-out refinance to consolidate his debt and improve his cash flow.

The lender reviews 12 months of Alex's personal bank statements and calculates a qualifying income of $20,000 per month. Based on his profile, Alex is approved for a cash-out refinance with a maximum loan-to-value ratio of 80%. This allows for a new loan amount of $520,000 on his $650,000 property. After paying off his existing mortgage of $300,000, Alex has $220,000 in available equity. After closing costs of $10,000, he receives $210,000 in cash.

Alex uses $80,000 of the cash-out proceeds to pay off all his high-interest debts: $40,000 in credit cards, $25,000 personal loan, and $15,000 business line of credit. This eliminates $2,180 in monthly payments. He allocates $50,000 to invest in his business, which he expects will increase his monthly income by $3,000 over time. He sets aside $30,000 as reserves and uses the remaining $50,000 to invest in a small rental property, generating $1,200 in monthly income.

The new mortgage is structured at $520,000 with a 6.5% interest rate, resulting in a monthly payment of approximately $3,300. While this is higher than his previous mortgage payment of $1,700, the overall financial picture has improved significantly. Alex's previous total monthly obligations were $3,880. After refinancing, his only major obligation is the $3,300 mortgage payment, as his other debts have been eliminated.

When factoring in the additional $1,200 in rental income, Alex's effective monthly obligation drops to $2,100 ($3,300 mortgage minus $1,200 rental income). This represents a reduction of $1,780 compared to his previous obligations. Additionally, as his business investment begins to generate an extra $3,000 per month, his cash flow improves even further.

Over time, Alex benefits from multiple layers of financial

improvement. His credit score increases as his credit card balances are paid off. His business grows, generating more income. His rental property appreciates and produces consistent cash flow. Meanwhile, his mortgage consolidates all his debt into a single, manageable payment. The $210,000 in equity that was once locked in his home has been transformed into a combination of debt elimination, income generation, and financial stability.

This example demonstrates how debt consolidation through bank statement refinancing can go beyond simply reducing payments. It can create a foundation for growth, improve financial efficiency, and unlock new opportunities. By understanding the numbers and applying a strategic approach, borrowers can turn a challenging financial situation into a powerful platform for long-term success.

Chapter 4

Liquidity Strategies and Building Financial Flexibility Through Bank Statement Refinancing

Liquidity is one of the most overlooked yet critical components of long-term financial success. Many borrowers focus on income, credit scores, and property values, but fail to recognize that access to cash—or the ability to quickly generate it—can determine whether opportunities are captured or missed. In real estate and business, timing is everything. Deals appear and disappear quickly, markets shift, and unexpected expenses arise. Without liquidity, even the most successful individuals can find themselves constrained, unable to act when it matters most. Bank statement refinancing, particularly through cash-out strategies, provides a powerful method for creating and maintaining liquidity without disrupting existing assets or relying on traditional income documentation.

At its core, liquidity is about flexibility. It is the ability to respond to opportunities, manage risk, and maintain control over your financial situation. For self-employed borrowers and investors, income can be variable, and access to traditional financing may be limited by tax return constraints. This makes liquidity even more valuable. By converting a portion of home equity into accessible cash, borrowers can create a financial buffer that supports both stability and growth. Unlike selling an asset, which eliminates future appreciation and income potential, refinancing allows borrowers to retain ownership while unlocking capital.

One of the primary advantages of liquidity through refinancing is the ability to act quickly on investment opportunities. In competitive real estate markets, properties with strong potential are often acquired by buyers who can move fast. Having cash readily available eliminates delays associated with securing financing, allowing borrowers to make competitive offers and close deals more efficiently. This speed can be the difference between acquiring a high-performing asset and missing out entirely. For investors, this advantage compounds over time, as each successful acquisition contributes to portfolio growth and income generation.

Liquidity also plays a critical role in risk management. Unexpected expenses—such as property repairs, vacancies, or economic downturns—can disrupt cash flow and create financial stress. Borrowers with adequate reserves are better positioned to navigate these challenges without resorting to high-interest debt or forced asset sales. By maintaining a portion of cash-out refinance proceeds as reserves, borrowers create a safety net that protects their financial stability. This approach reduces risk while preserving the ability to pursue growth opportunities.

Another key aspect of liquidity strategy is the concept of opportunity cost. Equity that remains locked in a property is essentially idle capital. While it contributes to net worth, it does not generate immediate income or provide flexibility. By accessing this equity through refinancing, borrowers can put that capital to work in ways that generate returns. This might include investing in additional properties, expanding a business, or entering new markets. The goal is to ensure that capital is actively contributing to financial growth rather than remaining dormant.

However, liquidity must be managed carefully to avoid over-leveraging. While accessing equity can create opportunities, it also increases the borrower's overall debt load. This makes it essential to balance liquidity with sustainability. Borrowers should evaluate their ability to service the new loan under various scenarios, including changes in income or market conditions. Maintaining conservative leverage ratios and adequate reserves helps ensure that liquidity enhances financial stability rather than introducing unnecessary risk. Bank statement loans provide a unique advantage in liquidity strategies because they allow borrowers to qualify based on actual cash flow rather than tax returns. This is particularly beneficial for entrepreneurs who reinvest heavily in their businesses or who have fluctuating income. By demonstrating consistent deposits and strong financial management, these borrowers can access refinancing options that would otherwise be unavailable. This flexibility enables more aggressive liquidity strategies while still maintaining a solid foundation for approval.

Strategic allocation of liquidity is just as important as accessing it. Once funds are obtained through a cash-out refinance, borrowers must decide how to deploy them effectively. This requires a clear understanding of financial goals and priorities. Some borrowers may choose to allocate funds toward income-generating investments, while others may focus on reducing risk or improving their financial position. In many cases, a balanced approach—combining investment, reserves, and debt reduction—provides the best outcome.

For real estate investors, liquidity can be used to accelerate portfolio growth. By using cash-out funds as down payments, investors can acquire additional properties without waiting to accumulate savings. This creates a cycle where each property contributes to the next, compounding growth over time. When combined with appreciation and rental income, this strategy can significantly increase net worth and cash flow. The key is to ensure that each investment meets specific criteria for profitability and risk management.

Liquidity can also be used to enhance existing assets. Property improvements, for example, can increase both value and rental income, creating additional equity and cash flow. This approach allows borrowers to maximize the performance of their current portfolio before expanding further. In some cases, improving existing properties may provide a higher return on investment than acquiring new ones. Evaluating these options requires careful analysis and a clear understanding of market conditions.

Another important consideration is maintaining liquidity for non-real estate opportunities. Business expansion, partnerships, and alternative investments can provide significant returns when approached strategically. Having access to capital allows borrowers to diversify their income streams and reduce reliance on a single source of income. This diversification enhances financial resilience and creates additional pathways for growth.

Timing plays a crucial role in liquidity strategies. Market conditions, interest rates, and property values all influence the effectiveness of a cash-out refinance. Borrowers should monitor these factors and be prepared to act when conditions are favorable. For example, rising property values can increase available equity, while stable interest rates can make refinancing more attractive. Understanding how these variables interact allows borrowers to make informed decisions and maximize the benefits of their strategy.

Ultimately, liquidity is about creating options. It is about having the ability to choose how and when to act, rather than being constrained by a lack of resources. Bank statement refinancing provides a pathway to achieve this flexibility, particularly for borrowers who do not fit traditional lending models. By combining this approach with strategic planning and disciplined execution, borrowers can build a financial structure that supports both stability and growth.

Real-Life Math Example: Building Liquidity and Expanding Opportunities

Let's go over a borrower named Daniel, a self-employed digital entrepreneur who owns a primary residence valued at $800,000 with a mortgage balance of $400,000. Daniel has experienced significant business growth over the past two years, with average monthly deposits of $25,000 reflected in his bank statements. However, due to business write-offs, his tax returns show a much lower income, limiting his ability to access traditional financing. Daniel decides to pursue a bank statement cash-out refinance to create liquidity and expand his investment opportunities. The lender reviews 24 months of Daniel's bank statements and calculates a qualifying income of $25,000 per month. Based on his profile, he is approved for a cash-out refinance with a maximum loan-to-value ratio of 75%. This allows for a new loan amount of $600,000 on his $800,000 property. After paying off his existing mortgage of $400,000, Daniel has $200,000 in available equity. After closing costs of $12,000, he receives $188,000 in cash.

Daniel develops a strategic plan for deploying this capital. He allocates $80,000 as reserves, ensuring he has a strong financial buffer for both personal and business needs. This reserve covers approximately 12 months of his mortgage payments, providing significant security. He uses $60,000 as a down payment on an investment property priced at $300,000. This property generates $2,200 per month in rental income, with a mortgage payment of $1,600, resulting in a net cash flow of $600 per month.

Daniel allocates another $30,000 to expand his business, investing in marketing and automation systems that increase his monthly revenue by $4,000 over time. The remaining $18,000 is used for minor renovations on his primary residence, increasing its value to $850,000. This not only enhances his living environment but also creates additional equity that can be accessed in the future. Daniel's new mortgage is structured at $600,000 with an interest rate of 6.5%, resulting in a monthly payment of approximately $3,800. His previous mortgage payment was $2,300, representing an increase of $1,500. However, this increase is offset by the additional income generated from his investments. The rental property provides $600 in net monthly income, and his business expansion adds $4,000 in monthly revenue.

When analyzing the numbers, Daniel's financial position improves significantly. His total additional income of $4,600 per month ($600 rental income + $4,000 business growth) exceeds the $1,500 increase in his mortgage payment. This results in a net positive cash flow increase of $3,100 per month. Additionally, he now has $80,000 in reserves, providing a strong safety net and enhancing his financial stability.

Over time, Daniel benefits from multiple layers of growth. His investment property appreciates in value, his business continues to generate higher income, and his primary residence increases in equity. The $188,000 in equity that was previously locked in his home has been transformed into a combination of liquidity, income generation, and financial security. This positions Daniel to pursue additional opportunities in the future, further compounding his wealth.

This example demonstrates how liquidity strategies, when combined with bank statement refinancing, can create a powerful foundation for both growth and stability. By accessing equity, maintaining reserves, and deploying capital strategically, borrowers can build a financial structure that supports long-term success while minimizing risk.

Chapter 5

Timing the Market, Interest Rates, and When to Execute a Bank Statement Refinance

Timing is one of the most critical—and often misunderstood—elements of a successful refinancing strategy. While many borrowers focus on loan structure, cash-out amounts, and qualification methods, the timing of when a refinance is executed can significantly influence both short-term outcomes and long-term financial performance. In the context of bank statement mortgage loans, timing becomes even more important because it intersects with multiple variables: interest rates, property values, income consistency, lender guidelines, and broader economic conditions. Understanding how to evaluate and align these factors can mean the difference between an average refinance and a highly optimized financial move.

At the center of timing decisions are interest rates. Mortgage rates fluctuate based on a variety of macroeconomic factors, including inflation, Federal Reserve policy, and bond market activity. Even small changes in interest rates can have a substantial impact on monthly payments and total loan costs.

For example, a difference of just 0.5% on a large loan amount can translate into hundreds of dollars per month and tens of thousands of dollars over the life of the loan. For borrowers considering a cash-out refinance, the decision to proceed must balance the cost of borrowing with the benefits of accessing equity.

However, interest rates alone should not dictate timing. A common mistake borrowers make is waiting indefinitely for the "perfect" rate, potentially missing out on opportunities to deploy capital effectively. The reality is that timing should be evaluated based on the overall financial outcome, not just the interest rate. If the funds obtained through refinancing can be used to generate returns that exceed the cost of borrowing, the refinance may still be beneficial even in a higher-rate environment. This perspective shifts the focus from cost minimization to value creation.

Property values are another key factor in timing a refinance. As property values increase, so does available equity. This creates opportunities for larger cash-out amounts and improved loan terms. In strong real estate markets, waiting for appreciation can enhance the benefits of refinancing. However, markets can also fluctuate, and delaying too long may expose borrowers to the risk of declining values. Understanding local market trends and positioning yourself to act when equity levels are favorable is an essential component of timing.

For bank statement loans, income consistency plays a unique role in timing decisions. Because lenders evaluate 12 to 24 months of bank statements, the borrower's recent financial activity directly impacts qualification. Borrowers who anticipate increased income may benefit from waiting until their bank statements reflect higher deposits. Conversely, those experiencing a temporary dip in income may choose to refinance before lower months are included in the evaluation period. This dynamic creates a strategic window where timing can be aligned with the strongest possible financial presentation.

Another important consideration is lender guideline changes. Non-QM and bank statement loan programs can evolve based on market conditions and investor appetite. Changes in maximum loan-to-value ratios, credit score requirements, or expense factor assumptions can influence qualification and loan terms. Borrowers who stay informed about these changes can take advantage of favorable guidelines when they are available. Working with knowledgeable professionals who understand the lending landscape can provide valuable insight into these shifts. Market cycles also play a role in refinancing strategy. Real estate and financial markets tend to move in cycles, influenced by economic growth, interest rates, and investor sentiment. During periods of expansion, property values and rental income may increase, creating opportunities for equity extraction and investment. During periods of contraction, liquidity and conservative leverage become more important. Timing a refinance within these cycles requires an understanding of where the market is and where it may be heading.

Break-even analysis is a practical tool for evaluating timing decisions. When refinancing, borrowers incur closing costs that must be offset by the financial benefits of the new loan. By calculating how long it will take for savings or income gains to exceed these costs, borrowers can determine whether a refinance makes sense. In cash-out scenarios, this analysis may include not only payment savings but also the returns generated from the use of funds. This broader perspective provides a more accurate assessment of the refinance's value.

Opportunity timing is another critical concept. In many cases, the best time to refinance is when a specific opportunity is available, rather than when market conditions are ideal. For example, if a borrower identifies a high-performing investment property or a business expansion opportunity with strong potential returns, accessing capital quickly may be more important than securing the lowest possible interest rate.

This requires a proactive approach to liquidity and a willingness to act when opportunities arise.

Risk tolerance also influences timing decisions. Some borrowers prefer to act conservatively, waiting for favorable conditions and minimizing risk. Others may take a more aggressive approach, leveraging opportunities even in less favorable environments. Understanding your own risk tolerance and aligning it with your financial goals is essential for making confident and effective decisions. There is no one-size-fits-all approach to timing; it must be tailored to the individual borrower's situation.

Another layer of timing involves future planning. Refinancing decisions should consider not only current conditions but also anticipated changes in income, expenses, and financial goals. For example, a borrower planning to expand their business or acquire additional properties may choose to refinance in advance to secure capital. Similarly, those expecting changes in income or credit profile may time their refinance to align with their strongest financial position.

Prepayment and exit strategies are also part of timing considerations. Borrowers should evaluate how long they plan to hold the loan and whether they intend to refinance again in the future. Understanding prepayment penalties, loan terms, and potential exit options allows borrowers to structure their refinance in a way that supports long-term flexibility. This forward-thinking approach ensures that current decisions do not limit future opportunities.

Ultimately, timing a bank statement refinance is about aligning multiple variables to achieve the best possible outcome. It requires a combination of market awareness, financial analysis, and strategic planning. By understanding how interest rates, property values, income trends, and opportunities interact, borrowers can position themselves to act at the right moment and maximize the benefits of their refinance.

Real-Life Math Example: Timing a Refinance for Maximum Financial Impact

For the next example, let's consider a borrower named Sophia, a self-employed marketing consultant who owns a primary residence valued at $750,000 with a current mortgage balance of $350,000 at an interest rate of 4.75%. Sophia's monthly mortgage payment is approximately $1,825. Over the past two years, her business has grown significantly, with average monthly deposits increasing from $15,000 to $24,000. However, her most recent six months show a strong upward trend, while earlier months reflect lower income levels.

Sophia is considering a cash-out refinance but must decide whether to proceed now or wait. Interest rates have recently increased, with current bank statement loan rates at approximately 6.5%. At the same time, property values in her area have risen, and her home is expected to appreciate further. Sophia evaluates her options carefully.

If Sophia refinances now, she qualifies based on her 24-month average income of approximately $19,500 per month. The lender allows a maximum loan-to-value ratio of 75%, resulting in a potential loan amount of $562,500 on her $750,000 property. After paying off her existing mortgage of $350,000, she would have $212,500 in available equity. After closing costs of $12,500, she would receive approximately $200,000 in cash.

Her new mortgage at 6.5% would result in a monthly payment of approximately $3,550, an increase of $1,725 compared to her current payment. Sophia plans to use the $200,000 to invest in two rental properties, each requiring $80,000 down, and allocate the remaining $40,000 as reserves. Each property is expected to generate $2,200 per month in rental income, with combined net cash flow of $1,200 after expenses.

Alternatively, Sophia considers waiting six months. By doing so, her 12-month bank statement average would increase to approximately $23,000 per month, improving her qualification profile. However, interest rates may rise further to 7%, and property values may increase to $780,000. Under this scenario, her maximum loan amount at 75% LTV would be $585,000. After paying off her mortgage, she would have $235,000 in equity, or approximately $220,000 after costs.

At a 7% interest rate, her new monthly payment would be approximately $3,900. While she would access an additional $20,000 in equity, her payment would be $350 higher than if she refinanced earlier. However, her stronger income profile could allow for more favorable underwriting and potentially better loan terms.

Sophia compares the two scenarios. Refinancing now provides immediate access to $200,000 and allows her to invest sooner, generating rental income earlier. Waiting increases her available equity but also increases her borrowing cost. By refinancing now, she begins generating $1,200 per month in rental income immediately, totaling $7,200 over six months. This offsets the benefit of waiting for additional equity.

Additionally, Sophia considers the potential appreciation of the investment properties. If each property increases in value by 3% annually, she gains approximately $9,000 in equity across both properties within the first year. This further supports the decision to act sooner rather than later.

After analyzing the numbers, Sophia decides to refinance now. While the interest rate is higher than her current loan, the ability to deploy capital immediately and generate income outweighs the cost of waiting. Her net financial position improves as the rental income offsets a significant portion of her increased mortgage payment, and she benefits from both cash flow and appreciation.

This example illustrates the importance of timing in refinancing decisions. By evaluating interest rates, property values, income trends, and opportunity costs, borrowers can make informed decisions that align with their financial goals. Timing is not about predicting the perfect moment—it is about understanding the trade-offs and acting when the overall outcome is favorable.

Chapter 6

Risk Management, Leverage, and Long-Term Sustainability in Bank Statement Refinancing

As powerful as bank statement refinancing and cash-out strategies can be, they must be approached with a disciplined understanding of risk and long-term sustainability. Many borrowers become focused on the opportunities created by accessing equity—investing, expanding, consolidating debt—but fail to fully account for the risks associated with increased leverage. The most successful borrowers are not those who simply maximize how much they can borrow, but those who understand how to balance opportunity with stability. In this chapter, we explore how to manage risk, use leverage intelligently, and build a financial structure that supports long-term success.

Leverage is the foundation of most real estate wealth-building strategies. It allows borrowers to control larger assets with relatively small amounts of capital, amplifying both returns and growth potential. However, leverage is a double-edged sword. While it can accelerate wealth creation in rising markets, it can also magnify losses in downturns or periods of financial instability. When using a bank statement cash-out refinance, borrowers are effectively increasing their leverage by taking on a larger loan balance. This makes it essential to evaluate not just the potential benefits, but also the ability to sustain the new debt under various scenarios.

One of the key principles of risk management is maintaining a margin of safety. This means ensuring that your financial structure can withstand unexpected changes, such as income fluctuations, interest rate increases, or declines in property values. For self-employed borrowers, whose income may vary from month to month, this is especially important. Bank statement loans provide flexibility in qualification, but they also require borrowers to be realistic about their ability to maintain consistent cash flow. Building a margin of safety involves conservative assumptions, adequate reserves, and a clear understanding of worst-case scenarios.

Cash reserves are one of the most effective tools for managing risk. After a cash-out refinance, it can be tempting to deploy all available funds into investments or other opportunities. However, maintaining a portion of those funds as reserves provides a buffer against unexpected expenses or income disruptions. Reserves can cover mortgage payments, property expenses, or business costs during challenging periods, reducing the need to rely on high-interest debt or liquidate assets under pressure. Lenders also view strong reserves as a positive compensating factor, which can improve loan terms and approval chances.

Another important aspect of risk management is diversification. Relying on a single source of income or a single type of investment increases vulnerability to market changes. By diversifying income streams—such as combining business income with rental income—borrowers create a more resilient financial structure. Similarly, diversifying investments across different property types, locations, or asset classes can reduce exposure to specific risks. Bank statement refinancing can facilitate this diversification by providing the capital needed to expand into new opportunities.

Debt-to-income management remains a critical factor, even in the context of bank statement loans. While these loans allow for more flexible income calculations, borrowers must still ensure that their overall debt obligations are manageable. A high debt-to-income ratio can limit future financing options and increase financial stress. By carefully structuring loans and maintaining a balance between income and obligations, borrowers can preserve their ability to access additional capital when needed.

Interest rate risk is another consideration in refinancing strategies. Many borrowers focus on current rates without considering how future rate changes might impact their financial position. While fixed-rate loans provide stability, borrowers who plan to refinance again or who hold multiple properties should be aware of how rising rates could affect their overall portfolio. Planning for different interest rate scenarios helps ensure that the strategy remains viable under changing conditions.

Property value fluctuations also play a role in risk management. Real estate markets are not static, and values can rise or fall based on economic conditions, supply and demand, and local factors. Borrowers who extract significant equity from their properties should be mindful of how declining values could impact their loan-to-value ratios and overall equity position. Maintaining a conservative approach to leverage helps protect against these fluctuations and preserves long-term flexibility.

Another key concept is the difference between productive and non-productive debt. Productive debt is used to generate income or create value, such as investing in rental properties or business expansion. Non-productive debt, on the other hand, does not generate returns and may simply increase financial burden. When using cash-out refinancing, borrowers should prioritize productive uses of capital whenever possible. This ensures that the additional debt contributes to financial growth rather than detracting from it. Scenario planning is an essential tool for evaluating risk. Borrowers should consider multiple scenarios, including best-case, expected, and worst-case outcomes. For example, what happens if rental income decreases? What if business revenue declines temporarily? What if unexpected expenses arise? By modeling these scenarios, borrowers can identify potential weaknesses in their strategy and make adjustments before problems occur. This proactive approach reduces uncertainty and increases confidence in decision-making.

Exit strategies are another important component of long-term sustainability. Borrowers should have a clear plan for how they will manage or exit their loans in the future. This may include refinancing again, selling a property, or paying down the loan over time. Understanding these options provides flexibility and ensures that current decisions do not limit future opportunities. For example, a borrower who plans to refinance again in a few years may structure their current loan differently than someone who intends to hold it long-term.

Behavioral discipline also plays a significant role in risk management. Access to large amounts of capital can create a temptation to overextend or pursue opportunities without

sufficient analysis. Successful borrowers maintain a disciplined approach, carefully evaluating each decision and aligning it with their long-term goals. This includes avoiding unnecessary spending, maintaining clear financial records, and continuously monitoring performance.

Bank statement refinancing, when used responsibly, can be a powerful tool for building wealth and achieving financial independence. However, its effectiveness depends on how it is implemented. By focusing on risk management, maintaining a margin of safety, and using leverage strategically, borrowers can create a financial structure that supports both growth and stability. The goal is not just to access capital, but to use it in a way that enhances long-term sustainability and resilience.

Real-Life Math Example: Balancing Leverage and Risk for Long-Term Stability

Consider a borrower named Kevin, a self-employed contractor who owns a primary residence valued at $700,000 with a mortgage balance of $300,000. Kevin's business generates an average of $22,000 per month in deposits, as reflected in his bank statements. He is considering a cash-out refinance to access equity and invest in additional properties. However, Kevin is also mindful of the risks associated with increased leverage and wants to ensure that his strategy is sustainable.

Kevin qualifies for a bank statement cash-out refinance with a maximum loan-to-value ratio of 75%, allowing for a new loan amount of $525,000. After paying off his existing mortgage of $300,000, he has $225,000 in available equity. After closing costs of $15,000, Kevin receives $210,000 in cash.

Rather than using all of the funds for investments, Kevin takes a balanced approach. He allocates $90,000 as reserves, covering approximately 12 months of mortgage payments and providing a strong safety net. He uses $80,000 as a down payment on an investment property priced at $400,000, which generates $2,400 per month in rental income. The mortgage payment on this property is $1,800, resulting in a net cash flow of $600 per month. The remaining $40,000 is used to pay off a portion of his existing debt and invest in business improvements that increase his monthly income by $2,000.

Kevin's new mortgage is structured at $525,000 with an interest rate of 6.75%, resulting in a monthly payment of approximately $3,400. His previous mortgage payment was $1,900, representing an increase of $1,500. However, this increase is offset by the additional income generated from his investments. The rental property provides $600 in net monthly income, and his business improvements add $2,000 per month.

When analyzing Kevin's financial position, his additional income of $2,600 per month exceeds the $1,500 increase in his mortgage payment, resulting in a net positive cash flow of $1,100 per month. Additionally, his $90,000 in reserves provides a significant buffer, reducing his exposure to risk.

Kevin also considers worst-case scenarios. If his rental property experiences a vacancy and generates no income for three months, he would lose $7,200 in expected income. However, his reserves are sufficient to cover this loss without impacting his financial stability. Similarly, if his business income temporarily decreases by $3,000 per month, he can rely on his reserves to maintain his obligations while adjusting his strategy.

Over time, Kevin's investment property appreciates in value, and his business continues to grow. His conservative approach to leverage allows him to benefit from these gains while minimizing risk. By maintaining reserves, diversifying income, and carefully evaluating each decision, Kevin creates a financial structure that supports both growth and stability.

This example demonstrates how risk management and leverage can be balanced effectively in a bank statement refinancing strategy. By taking a disciplined approach and planning for multiple scenarios, borrowers can use refinancing as a tool for long-term success rather than short-term gain.

Chapter 7

Structuring the Perfect Bank Statement Cash-Out Refinance for Maximum Approval and Profitability

As you progress through the strategies of bank statement refinancing, one principle becomes increasingly clear: success is not just about accessing equity—it is about how you structure the loan. Two borrowers with identical properties, income, and credit profiles can receive very different outcomes depending on how their loan is presented, documented, and aligned with lender guidelines. Structuring is the difference between an approval and a denial, between an average deal and a highly optimized one. In this chapter, we focus on how to engineer the perfect bank statement cash-out refinance to maximize both approval odds and long-term profitability.

The first element of structuring is understanding how lenders view risk. Every loan is evaluated through a lens of risk assessment, where factors such as income stability, credit profile, property type, reserves, and loan-to-value ratio all contribute to the overall picture. Bank statement loans provide flexibility, but they still require a cohesive and logical financial story. The borrower's file must demonstrate not only the ability to repay the loan but also consistency and reliability. This means structuring your finances in a way that aligns with how lenders analyze bank statements and cash flow.

Income presentation is one of the most critical components of structuring. Unlike traditional loans that rely on tax returns, bank statement loans focus on deposits. However, not all deposits are treated equally. Lenders look for recurring, consistent deposits that clearly represent income. Large one-time deposits, transfers between accounts, or undocumented funds can raise questions and potentially reduce qualifying income. Borrowers who understand this can take proactive steps—such as separating personal and business accounts, maintaining consistent deposit patterns, and avoiding unnecessary transfers—to create a cleaner and more favorable income profile.

The choice between personal and business bank statements is another key structuring decision. Personal bank statements often allow for 100% of eligible deposits to be used as income, while business bank statements typically require an expense factor to account for operational costs. In some cases, using personal statements may result in higher qualifying income, while in others, a well-documented business account with a CPA-prepared profit and loss statement may provide a more accurate representation. The decision should be based on which option presents the strongest and most consistent financial picture.

Expense factor optimization is a powerful tool in structuring business bank statement loans. Lenders may apply standard expense ratios—such as 50%—to business deposits unless a CPA provides documentation supporting a lower ratio. By working with a CPA to prepare a profit and loss statement, borrowers can potentially reduce the expense factor to 10%, 15%, or 20%, significantly increasing qualifying income. This can have a direct impact on loan approval and maximum loan amount, making it a critical consideration in the structuring process.

Loan-to-value ratio (LTV) is another central element of structuring. While it may be tempting to maximize cash-out by borrowing up to the highest allowable LTV, doing so can increase risk and potentially limit approval options. Lower LTVs generally result in better pricing, lower interest rates, and stronger approval profiles. In some cases, reducing the loan amount slightly can lead to significantly better terms. Borrowers should evaluate the trade-off between accessing additional cash and securing more favorable loan conditions.

Credit profile optimization also plays a major role in structuring. While bank statement loans are more flexible than traditional loans, credit scores still influence interest rates, LTV limits, and overall approval. Paying down credit card balances, correcting errors on credit reports, and maintaining on-time payment history can improve credit scores and enhance loan terms. Even small improvements in credit can lead to meaningful savings over the life of the loan.

Reserves are one of the most underrated yet impactful components of a strong loan structure. Lenders view reserves as a safety net that reduces risk, particularly for self-employed borrowers. Demonstrating several months of mortgage payments in reserves can strengthen the file and potentially offset other weaknesses. In some cases, higher reserves can lead to higher allowable LTVs or more favorable pricing. Structuring your refinance to include and preserve reserves is a key strategy for both approval and long-term stability.

Debt-to-income ratio (DTI) must also be carefully managed. While bank statement loans allow for more flexibility in income calculation, lenders still evaluate the relationship between income and obligations. Structuring the loan to maintain a reasonable DTI ensures that the borrower can comfortably manage the new payment. This may involve paying off certain debts, adjusting the loan amount, or selecting a loan term that balances payment and cost. Another advanced structuring technique involves layering strategies.

For example, a borrower may combine a cash-out refinance with debt consolidation, reserve allocation, and investment planning. By addressing multiple objectives within a single transaction, the borrower can maximize the impact of the refinance. This requires careful planning and a clear understanding of priorities, but it can significantly enhance the overall outcome.

Property type and usage also influence structuring decisions. Primary residences, second homes, and investment properties each have different guidelines, LTV limits, and risk profiles. Understanding these differences allows borrowers to choose the most advantageous approach. For example, refinancing a primary residence may allow for higher LTVs and better pricing, while investment properties may offer greater income potential. Structuring decisions should align with both immediate goals and long-term strategy.

Timing within the structuring process is equally important. Preparing your financial profile in advance—organizing bank statements, reducing unnecessary expenses, and stabilizing income—can improve the strength of your application. Borrowers who take the time to prepare before applying are more likely to achieve favorable outcomes. This proactive approach is a hallmark of successful refinancing strategies.

Communication and presentation are the final elements of structuring. A well-prepared file tells a clear and compelling story. This includes organized documentation, consistent financial records, and a logical explanation of any anomalies. Working with experienced professionals who understand bank statement lending can further enhance this presentation, ensuring that the borrower's strengths are highlighted and potential concerns are addressed.

Ultimately, structuring is about control. It is about taking an active role in shaping the outcome of your refinance rather than leaving it to chance. By understanding how lenders evaluate risk and aligning your financial profile accordingly, you can significantly increase your chances of approval and optimize the terms of your loan. This level of control transforms refinancing from a reactive process into a strategic tool for building wealth and achieving financial goals.

Real-Life Math Example: Engineering a High-Approval, High-Return Cash-Out Refinance

Now, let's talk about a borrower named Laura, a self-employed interior designer who owns a primary residence valued at $900,000 with a mortgage balance of $400,000. Laura's business generates strong revenue, with average monthly deposits of $30,000 across her bank accounts. However, her income fluctuates slightly due to seasonal projects, and her tax returns show lower net income due to deductions. Laura wants to structure a bank statement cash-out refinance that maximizes her approval chances while also providing capital for investment.

Laura begins by organizing her financial profile. She separates her personal and business accounts, ensuring that her income deposits are clearly identifiable and consistent. She works with her CPA to prepare a profit and loss statement, reducing her expense factor from the lender's standard 50% to 20%. This significantly increases her qualifying income. With $30,000 in monthly deposits and a 20% expense factor, her qualifying income is calculated at $24,000 per month.

The lender approves Laura for a cash-out refinance with a maximum LTV of 75%, allowing for a loan amount of $675,000 on her $900,000 property. After paying off her existing mortgage of $400,000, she has $275,000 in available equity. After closing costs of $15,000, Laura receives $260,000 in cash.

Rather than maximizing leverage, Laura chooses a slightly lower loan amount of $650,000 to improve her loan terms and reduce risk. This results in a cash-out amount of $250,000 after costs. Her new mortgage at 6.5% results in a monthly payment of approximately $4,100, compared to her previous payment of $2,200.

Laura allocates the $250,000 strategically. She uses $120,000 as down payments on two investment properties, each priced at $300,000. These properties generate $2,400 per month each in rental income, for a total of $4,800. The combined mortgage payments on these properties are $3,200, resulting in net cash flow of $1,600 per month. She allocates $80,000 as reserves, covering nearly 20 months of her new mortgage payments, and uses the remaining $50,000 to invest in her business, increasing her monthly income by $3,000.

When analyzing the numbers, Laura's new mortgage payment increases by $1,900 ($4,100 new payment minus $2,200 old payment). However, her additional rental income of $1,600 and business income increase of $3,000 result in a total income increase of $4,600 per month. After offsetting the higher mortgage payment, Laura achieves a net positive cash flow increase of $2,700 per month.

Additionally, Laura's total real estate portfolio value increases from $900,000 to $1.5 million, and she maintains strong reserves that reduce her financial risk. Her improved credit profile, consistent income presentation, and strategic allocation of funds position her for future refinancing opportunities and continued growth.

This example demonstrates how proper structuring can significantly enhance both approval and profitability. By optimizing income presentation, managing leverage, maintaining reserves, and aligning the loan with clear financial goals, Laura transforms her refinance into a powerful wealth-building strategy.

Chapter 8

Exit Strategies, Portfolio Optimization, and Long-Term Wealth Creation

As you reach this stage of mastering bank statement refinancing and cash-out strategies, it becomes essential to shift your focus from short-term execution to long-term outcomes. Accessing equity, consolidating debt, and increasing liquidity are powerful steps, but they are only part of a larger financial journey. True success comes from understanding how to manage, optimize, and eventually exit or reposition your portfolio in a way that maximizes wealth while minimizing risk. This chapter is about thinking beyond the transaction—about building a system that evolves over time and continues to create value long after the refinance is complete.

An exit strategy is not about leaving real estate or eliminating debt entirely. It is about having a clear plan for how each financial decision contributes to your long-term goals. Every refinance, every investment, and every allocation of capital should be aligned with a broader vision. This might include building passive income, achieving financial independence, creating generational wealth, or transitioning into a more conservative financial position later in life. Without an exit strategy, even the most successful short-term moves can lead to inefficiencies or missed opportunities.

One of the most common exit strategies involves refinancing again in the future under more favorable conditions. Bank statement loans provide flexibility for qualification, but they often come with slightly higher interest rates than traditional loans. As a borrower's financial profile improves—through increased income, higher credit scores, or stronger documented earnings—it may become possible to transition into a conventional or lower-rate loan. This strategy allows borrowers to benefit from the flexibility of bank statement loans initially, while planning for improved terms over time.

Another exit approach is the gradual reduction of leverage. While leverage is a powerful tool for growth, there comes a point where reducing debt can enhance stability and increase net income. This may involve making extra principal payments, refinancing into shorter-term loans, or selling underperforming assets to pay down balances. The goal is to strike a balance between growth and security, ensuring that your portfolio continues to generate income while reducing exposure to risk.

Portfolio optimization is the process of evaluating and improving the performance of your assets over time. Not all properties or investments will perform equally, and part of long-term success involves identifying which assets to hold, improve, refinance, or sell. For example, a property with strong appreciation potential but low cash flow may be suitable for long-term holding, while a property with declining performance may be better repositioned or replaced. Bank statement refinancing can play a role in this process by providing the capital needed to upgrade, reposition, or exit certain investments.

A key concept in portfolio optimization is return on equity. As properties appreciate and equity increases, the return generated on that equity may decrease if income does not grow proportionally. In such cases, refinancing or selling the property to redeploy capital into higher-yield opportunities can improve overall portfolio performance. This requires a willingness to evaluate assets objectively and make decisions based on performance rather than emotional attachment.

Cash flow remains a central focus in long-term wealth creation. While appreciation contributes to net worth, consistent cash flow provides financial stability and supports ongoing growth. A well-structured portfolio balances both elements, ensuring that properties generate sufficient income to cover expenses, service debt, and provide surplus cash for reinvestment. Bank statement refinancing can be used to enhance cash flow by restructuring debt, consolidating obligations, or funding improvements that increase rental income.

Tax efficiency is another important consideration in long-term strategy. Real estate offers numerous tax advantages, including depreciation, expense deductions, and potential capital gains benefits. Refinancing can also play a role in tax planning, as cash-out proceeds are generally not considered taxable income. By working with knowledgeable professionals, borrowers can structure their strategies in a way that maximizes after-tax returns and aligns with their overall financial plan.

Market cycles and timing continue to influence long-term decisions. As markets evolve, opportunities and risks shift. Periods of rapid appreciation may present opportunities to extract equity or sell assets, while periods of stabilization may favor holding and optimizing cash flow. Understanding these cycles allows borrowers to adapt their strategies and make informed decisions that align with current conditions.

Legacy planning is an often-overlooked aspect of long-term wealth creation. For many borrowers, real estate is not just a source of income but a means of creating generational wealth. This involves considering how assets will be managed, transferred, or leveraged in the future. Structuring properties within appropriate ownership entities, maintaining clear records, and planning for succession are all part of this process. Bank statement refinancing can support legacy planning by providing the flexibility needed to adapt to changing circumstances.

Another advanced strategy involves portfolio consolidation or expansion. As borrowers gain experience and confidence, they may choose to consolidate smaller properties into larger, more efficient assets or expand into new markets and asset classes. This requires a clear understanding of risk, return, and operational considerations. The ability to access capital through refinancing provides the flexibility needed to execute these strategies effectively.

Exit strategies also include the potential sale of assets. Selling a property can provide liquidity, reduce risk, or allow for the reallocation of capital into higher-performing investments. The decision to sell should be based on a comprehensive analysis of market conditions, property performance, and long-term goals. In some cases, a partial exit—such as selling one property while retaining others—can achieve the desired balance between liquidity and growth.

Behavioral discipline remains critical throughout the

long-term process. Markets will fluctuate, opportunities will vary, and financial conditions will change. Maintaining a disciplined approach—focused on data, strategy, and long-term goals—ensures that decisions are made rationally rather than emotionally. This discipline is what separates sustainable success from short-term gains.

Ultimately, the goal of bank statement refinancing and cash-out strategies is not just to access capital, but to create a system that supports ongoing growth, stability, and flexibility. By integrating exit strategies, portfolio optimization, and long-term planning, borrowers can transform individual transactions into a cohesive financial strategy. This approach allows you to not only build wealth, but to manage and preserve it over time.

Real-Life Math Example: Building, Optimizing, and Exiting a High-Performance Portfolio

Now, let's talk a borrower named Michael, a self-employed consultant who has built a portfolio of three properties over several years. His primary residence is valued at $800,000 with a mortgage balance of $400,000. He owns two investment properties: Property A valued at $500,000 with a mortgage of $300,000, and Property B valued at $450,000 with a mortgage of $280,000. Michael's total portfolio value is

$1,750,000, with total debt of $980,000, resulting in $770,000 in equity.

Michael's bank statements show consistent monthly deposits of $28,000, allowing him to qualify for a bank statement cash-out refinance. He decides to refinance his primary residence at a 75% LTV, resulting in a new loan amount of $600,000. After paying off his existing mortgage, he accesses $200,000 in equity, receiving approximately $185,000 after closing costs.

Michael uses $100,000 of the funds to acquire a fourth investment property priced at $400,000, generating $2,600 per month in rental income with a mortgage payment of $1,900, resulting in $700 in net cash flow. He allocates $50,000 to renovate Property B, increasing its value to $520,000 and raising rental income from $2,200 to $2,800 per month, adding $600 in monthly cash flow. The remaining $35,000 is held as reserves.

After these changes, Michael's portfolio value increases to $2,120,000, and his total rental income rises significantly. Property A generates $2,500 per month with a $1,800 payment, netting $700. Property B now generates $2,800 with a $1,900 payment, netting $900. The new property generates

$700 in net cash flow. In total, Michael's rental income produces $2,300 in monthly net cash flow.

Michael's new mortgage on his primary residence is $600,000 at 6.5%, resulting in a monthly payment of approximately $3,800, compared to his previous payment of $2,300. This is an increase of $1,500. However, his additional rental income of $1,300 ($2,300 new total minus $1,000 previous total) offsets most of this increase, resulting in a manageable net change. Over the next five years, Michael evaluates his portfolio performance. Property B, after renovations, appreciates significantly and reaches a value of $650,000. He decides to sell this property, realizing a gain of $130,000 after expenses. He uses these proceeds to pay down the mortgage on his primary residence, reducing his balance to $470,000 and lowering his monthly payment.

At the same time, his other properties continue to generate income and appreciate. His portfolio remains diversified, with strong cash flow and reduced overall leverage. By strategically refinancing, investing, improving, and eventually selling one asset, Michael optimizes his portfolio and strengthens his financial position.

This example illustrates how bank statement refinancing can be integrated into a long-term strategy that includes growth, optimization, and exit planning. By understanding how to manage each stage of the process, borrowers can create a dynamic financial system that adapts over time and continues to generate value.

Chapter 9

Overcoming Credit Challenges and Structuring Strong Approvals with Bank Statement Loans

One of the most powerful advantages of bank statement mortgage loans is their ability to provide financing solutions for borrowers who do not fit traditional lending models. While much of the discussion around these programs focuses on income flexibility, another equally important benefit is their adaptability when dealing with credit challenges. Many self-employed borrowers, entrepreneurs, and investors have experienced financial events that impact their credit profiles—such as late payments, high utilization, collections, or even major events like foreclosures or bankruptcies. Traditional lending often treats these issues as disqualifying factors, but bank statement loans offer a pathway to approval when structured correctly.

Credit challenges do not define a borrower's current financial strength. In many cases, they are the result of past circumstances—business investments, market downturns, or temporary cash flow disruptions. What matters most to lenders is not just what happened, but how the borrower has recovered. Bank statement loans place greater emphasis on recent financial behavior, cash flow consistency, and overall financial stability. This allows borrowers to present a more accurate and current picture of their financial situation, rather than being judged solely on historical credit events.

Understanding how lenders evaluate credit is the first step in overcoming challenges. Credit scores are a summary of various factors, including payment history, credit utilization, length of credit history, and types of credit. While bank statement lenders may accept lower credit scores than traditional programs, the score still influences loan terms, interest rates, and maximum loan-to-value ratios. Borrowers with lower scores may face higher rates or reduced LTV limits, but approval is often still achievable with the right compensating factors.

Compensating factors are the key to structuring strong approvals in the presence of credit challenges. These factors demonstrate strength in other areas of the borrower's profile and help offset perceived risk. Common compensating factors include high income relative to the loan amount, significant cash reserves, low loan-to-value ratios, strong rental income, or a history of consistent bank deposits. By emphasizing these strengths, borrowers can create a balanced profile that supports approval despite credit imperfections. One of the most effective strategies for improving approval odds is reducing credit utilization before applying for a loan. High credit card balances can significantly lower credit scores and raise concerns about financial management. Paying down these balances—even partially—can lead to immediate improvements in credit scores and overall loan terms. This is a relatively simple step that can have a substantial impact on the outcome of a refinance.

Seasoning of credit events is another important factor. Lenders typically require a certain amount of time to pass after major credit events such as bankruptcies, foreclosures, or short sales. This period, known as seasoning, demonstrates that the borrower has had time to recover and reestablish financial stability. Bank statement loan programs often have more flexible seasoning requirements than traditional loans, allowing borrowers to qualify sooner. Understanding these timelines and planning accordingly can help borrowers position themselves for approval at the right time.

Documentation and explanation also play a critical role in overcoming credit challenges. Borrowers should be prepared to provide clear and concise explanations for any negative credit events, along with supporting documentation if necessary. This helps lenders understand the context and assess whether the issues are likely to recur. A well-documented explanation can turn a potential red flag into a manageable aspect of the overall profile. Structuring the loan with a lower loan-to-value ratio is another effective approach. By reducing the amount borrowed relative to the property value, borrowers decrease the lender's risk exposure. This can lead to improved approval chances and better loan terms, even with lower credit scores. In some cases, bringing additional funds to closing or limiting the cash-out amount can make a significant difference in the strength of the application.

Reserves become even more important when dealing with credit challenges. Demonstrating several months—or even a year—of mortgage payments in reserves shows that the borrower has the financial capacity to handle unexpected situations. This provides reassurance to lenders and strengthens the overall profile. For borrowers with lower credit scores, strong reserves can be a decisive factor in securing approval.

Income consistency remains a cornerstone of bank statement loan qualification. Even if credit is less than perfect, consistent and well-documented bank deposits can demonstrate the borrower's ability to repay the loan. Lenders are particularly interested in stability—regular deposits over time that indicate a reliable income stream. Borrowers who can present this consistency have a strong advantage, regardless of credit history. Another advanced strategy involves layering improvements before applying for a refinance. This might include paying down debt, increasing reserves, stabilizing income, and allowing time for credit scores to improve. By taking a proactive approach, borrowers can significantly enhance their profiles and secure better loan terms. This preparation phase is often the difference between a marginal approval and an optimal one.

Interest rate considerations are also important. Borrowers with credit challenges may receive higher interest rates due to increased risk. However, this does not mean the refinance is not beneficial. As discussed in previous chapters, the value of a refinance should be evaluated based on the overall financial outcome. If the funds obtained are used to generate income, reduce high-interest debt, or create opportunities, the benefits may outweigh the higher rate. Additionally, borrowers can plan to refinance again in the future as their credit improves.

Psychological factors should not be overlooked. Credit challenges can create hesitation or a lack of confidence in pursuing financing. However, understanding that there are viable solutions—and that lenders are willing to work with borrowers who demonstrate strength in other areas—can empower individuals to take action. Confidence, combined with preparation and strategy, is a powerful combination.

Ultimately, overcoming credit challenges in bank statement refinancing is about shifting the focus from limitations to possibilities. It is about understanding how to present a complete and compelling financial picture, leveraging strengths, and structuring the loan in a way that aligns with lender expectations. By doing so, borrowers can access the capital they need to move forward, regardless of past setbacks.

Real-Life Math Example: Turning Credit Challenges into a Strategic Advantage

Let's review a borrower named Jason, a self-employed restaurant owner who has experienced both success and setbacks. Jason owns a primary residence valued at $650,000 with a mortgage balance of $300,000. He also carries $50,000 in credit card debt and has a credit score of 640 due to past late payments during a slow business period. Despite these challenges, Jason's business has recovered, and his bank statements show consistent deposits averaging $21,000 per month over the past 12 months.

Jason decides to pursue a bank statement cash-out refinance to consolidate his debt and improve his financial position. The lender evaluates his profile and approves him for a loan with a maximum loan-to-value ratio of 70%, slightly lower than the standard 75% due to his credit score. This results in a maximum loan amount of $455,000 on his $650,000 property. After paying off his existing mortgage of $300,000, Jason has $155,000 in available equity. After closing costs of $10,000, he receives $145,000 in cash. Jason uses $50,000 to pay off his credit card debt, eliminating monthly payments of approximately $1,200. He allocates $40,000 to renovate his restaurant, increasing monthly revenue by $3,500 over time. He sets aside $30,000 as reserves and uses the remaining $25,000 as a down payment on a small rental property.

The rental property generates $1,400 per month in income with a mortgage payment of $1,000, resulting in $400 in net cash flow. Jason's new mortgage is $455,000 at an interest rate of 7%, resulting in a monthly payment of approximately $3,000, compared to his previous payment of $1,800. This is an increase of $1,200.

However, Jason's financial picture improves significantly. By eliminating his $1,200 credit card payment, he offsets the increase in his mortgage payment. Additionally, his rental property generates $400 in net income, and his restaurant improvements add $3,500 in monthly revenue. Even after accounting for business expenses, this results in a substantial increase in overall cash flow.

Over time, Jason's credit score improves as his credit card balances are paid off and his payment history stabilizes.

Within 12 to 18 months, his score increases to 700, allowing him to refinance again at a lower interest rate. This reduces his monthly payment and further improves his financial position.

Jason's initial refinance, despite higher rates and credit challenges, serves as a turning point. It allows him to eliminate high-interest debt, invest in his business, and begin building additional income streams. By structuring the loan strategically and leveraging compensating factors, he transforms a challenging financial situation into a pathway for growth.

This example demonstrates that credit challenges do not have to be barriers to success. With the right strategy, preparation, and understanding of bank statement loan programs, borrowers can overcome obstacles and create opportunities for long-term financial improvement.

Chapter 10

Advanced Bank Statement Loan Structuring—Engineering Approvals Using Deposits, Expense Ratios, and Investor Guidelines

At the highest level of mastery, bank statement mortgage loans are no longer just a financing option—they become a system that can be engineered with precision. The difference between an average borrower and a highly strategic borrower lies in understanding how to control the variables that lenders use to evaluate a file. Deposits, expense ratios, account structuring, timing, reserves, and investor overlays are not random factors—they are levers that can be adjusted to create stronger approvals, larger loan amounts, and more favorable terms. In this final chapter, we focus on advanced structuring techniques that allow you to design your loan outcome rather than simply accept it.

The foundation of advanced structuring begins with deposit engineering. Since bank statement loans rely heavily on deposits to determine income, the way deposits are received, categorized, and presented can significantly impact qualification. Lenders prefer consistent, recurring deposits that clearly represent income. This means that borrowers should aim to create predictable patterns in their accounts. For example, instead of receiving irregular lump sums, structuring deposits into consistent weekly or monthly amounts can create a smoother income profile. This consistency reduces perceived risk and increases qualifying income stability.

Another key aspect of deposit engineering is separating business and personal finances. Borrowers who mix accounts often create confusion in the underwriting process, as lenders must differentiate between business revenue, transfers, and personal income. By maintaining clean, separate accounts, borrowers can present a clear financial picture that supports their application. In some cases, using personal accounts may result in higher qualifying income, while in others, business accounts—supported by a CPA-prepared profit and loss statement—may provide better results. The choice should be strategic, based on which structure produces the strongest outcome.

Expense ratio optimization is one of the most powerful tools in advanced structuring. When lenders analyze business bank statements, they often apply a default expense ratio—commonly 50%—to account for operating costs. This can significantly reduce qualifying income. However, by providing a CPA-prepared profit and loss statement, borrowers can often reduce this ratio to 10%, 15%, or 20%. For example, if a borrower has $40,000 in monthly business deposits, a 50% expense ratio results in $20,000 of qualifying income, while a 20% ratio results in $32,000. This difference can dramatically increase borrowing capacity and improve loan terms.

Layering income sources is another advanced technique. Borrowers with multiple streams of income—such as business revenue, rental income, or side ventures—can combine these sources to strengthen their overall profile. Bank statement loans allow for flexibility in how income is calculated, and properly documenting multiple streams can create a more robust financial picture. This diversification not only improves qualification but also demonstrates stability, which is highly valued by lenders.

Investor guidelines and overlays add another layer of complexity and opportunity. Different lenders and investors have varying criteria for bank statement loans, including differences in allowable loan-to-value ratios, credit score requirements, and reserve expectations. Understanding these differences allows borrowers to match their profiles with the most favorable programs. For example, one lender may allow 80% LTV with strong reserves, while another may cap at 70%

but offer better pricing. Selecting the right lender is as important as structuring the loan itself.

Advanced structuring also involves optimizing loan size and pricing tiers. Interest rates and fees often vary based on loan amount, credit score, and LTV. In some cases, slightly reducing the loan amount can move the borrower into a more favorable pricing tier, resulting in lower interest rates and long-term savings. This requires a detailed analysis of trade-offs, balancing immediate cash-out needs with overall cost efficiency.

Reserves continue to play a critical role at this level. Beyond meeting minimum requirements, strategic borrowers use reserves as a tool to enhance their profile. Demonstrating 12, 18, or even 24 months of reserves can significantly reduce perceived risk and improve loan terms. In some cases, higher reserves can compensate for lower credit scores or higher LTVs, creating a more balanced and approvable file.

Timing and sequencing are also essential in advanced structuring. Borrowers may choose to prepare their financial profile over several months before applying for a refinance. This could include stabilizing deposits, reducing expenses, paying down debt, and increasing reserves. By controlling the timing of the application, borrowers ensure that their bank statements reflect their strongest possible financial position. Another advanced strategy involves structuring for future refinances. A borrower may initially use a bank statement loan to access capital and execute a strategy, with the intention of refinancing into a lower-rate conventional loan later. This requires planning from the outset, ensuring that the current loan supports future transitions. Factors such as prepayment penalties, loan terms, and anticipated income changes must be considered.

Portfolio-level structuring is the next level of sophistication. Borrowers with multiple properties can evaluate their entire portfolio and decide which assets to refinance, which to hold, and which to reposition. For example, refinancing a primary residence may provide better terms and higher LTV, while investment properties may offer stronger income potential. By strategically selecting which assets to leverage, borrowers can optimize their overall financial structure.

Another key concept is capital velocity—the speed at which capital is deployed and redeployed to generate returns. Advanced borrowers focus on minimizing idle capital and maximizing the productivity of their funds. This may involve refinancing, investing, improving properties, and repeating the process over time. The goal is to create a cycle where capital continuously generates value.

Risk-adjusted returns become increasingly important as strategies become more complex. Borrowers must evaluate not only potential returns but also the risks associated with each decision. This includes analyzing cash flow stability, market conditions, and leverage levels. By balancing risk and return, borrowers can create a sustainable strategy that supports long-term growth.

Behavioral discipline remains the foundation of all advanced strategies. Access to large amounts of capital and complex structuring options can create opportunities, but also risks. Maintaining a disciplined approach—focused on data, planning, and long-term goals—ensures that decisions are made strategically rather than impulsively.

Ultimately, advanced bank statement loan structuring is about control and precision. It is about understanding the system well enough to design outcomes that align with your goals. By mastering these techniques, borrowers can move beyond basic refinancing and create a financial framework that supports ongoing growth, flexibility, and wealth creation.

Real-Life Math Example: Engineering a High-Level Bank Statement Loan Strategy

Let's go over a borrower named Daniel, a self-employed consultant with multiple income streams and a growing real estate portfolio. Daniel has monthly business deposits of \$45,000 and rental income of \$5,000 per month. His primary residence is valued at \$1,000,000 with a mortgage balance of \$500,000. He wants to structure a cash-out refinance to maximize both approval and long-term returns.

Daniel works with his CPA to prepare a profit and loss statement, reducing his expense ratio from 50% to 20%. This results in qualifying income of \$36,000 from business deposits (\$45,000 × 80%) plus \$5,000 in rental income, for a total of \$41,000 per month. This strong income profile allows him to qualify for a higher loan amount.

The lender offers a maximum LTV of 75%, resulting in a potential loan amount of \$750,000. However, Daniel strategically chooses a loan amount of \$720,000 to secure better pricing and reduce risk. After paying off his existing mortgage, he accesses \$220,000 in equity, receiving approximately \$205,000 after closing costs.

Daniel allocates the funds strategically. He uses \$120,000 as down payments on two investment properties, each priced at \$400,000. These properties generate \$2,800 per month each in rental income, for a total of \$5,600. The combined mortgage payments are \$3,800, resulting in \$1,800 in net cash flow. He allocates \$50,000 as reserves, covering more than a year of mortgage payments, and uses the remaining $35,000 to invest in his business, increasing monthly income by $4,000. Daniel's new mortgage is $720,000 at 6.25%, resulting in a monthly payment of approximately $4,400, compared to his previous payment of $2,800. This is an increase of $1,600. However, his additional rental income of $1,800 and business income increase of $4,000 result in a total income increase of $5,800 per month.

After offsetting the higher mortgage payment, Daniel achieves a net positive cash flow increase of $4,200 per month. Additionally, his total real estate portfolio value increases significantly, and his reserves provide a strong safety net.

Daniel also plans for the future. As his business continues to grow and his credit profile strengthens, he intends to refinance into a lower-rate loan within two years, reducing his monthly payment and further improving cash flow. This forward-thinking approach ensures that his current strategy supports long-term optimization.

This example illustrates how advanced structuring can transform a refinance into a highly efficient financial system. By optimizing deposits, reducing expense ratios, layering income, and aligning with investor guidelines, Daniel maximizes both approval and profitability while maintaining control over risk and future opportunities.

Chapter 11

Building a Repeatable System—Scaling Bank Statement Refinancing for Ongoing Wealth Creation

At this stage, you are no longer simply learning how to refinance—you are learning how to build a system. The true power of bank statement mortgage loans is not found in a single transaction, but in the ability to repeat, refine, and scale the strategy over time. The most successful borrowers think in cycles, not events. They understand that refinancing, investing, improving, and repositioning assets can be done again and again, creating a compounding effect that accelerates wealth creation. In this chapter, we focus on how to turn everything you have learned into a repeatable, scalable system that can be applied consistently for long-term growth.

The foundation of a repeatable system begins with clarity of process. Every successful borrower follows a cycle: build equity, access equity, deploy capital, increase income, and repeat. This cycle is not theoretical—it is practical and measurable. As equity grows through appreciation and loan paydown, it creates the opportunity for refinancing. The funds obtained are then deployed into investments or improvements that generate income or increase value. This additional income strengthens the borrower's financial profile, making it easier to qualify for future refinances. Over time, this creates a feedback loop where each step reinforces the next.

Consistency is the key to making this system work. Lenders evaluate bank statements over specific time periods, typically 12 or 24 months. Borrowers who maintain consistent deposits, stable financial patterns, and organized accounts position themselves for ongoing access to financing. This means treating your financial profile as an asset that must be managed and maintained. Regular deposits, clear documentation, and disciplined financial behavior are not just good practices—they are strategic tools that support the entire system.

One of the most important aspects of scaling is understanding capital recycling. When you refinance and extract equity, you are not just accessing cash—you are repositioning capital. That capital can then be used to acquire new assets, improve existing ones, or create additional income streams. As those investments perform, they generate both income and equity, which can be accessed again in the future. This process allows you to grow your portfolio without relying solely on savings or external funding. Another key component is portfolio tracking and performance measurement. As your portfolio grows, it becomes increasingly important to monitor the performance of each asset. This includes tracking rental income, expenses, appreciation, and overall return on investment. By analyzing this data, you can identify which assets are performing well and which may need to be repositioned or replaced. This level of awareness allows you to make informed decisions and continuously optimize your portfolio.

Scaling also requires an understanding of operational efficiency. Managing multiple properties or investments can become complex, and inefficiencies can erode profitability. Systems for property management, financial tracking, and maintenance must be streamlined to ensure that growth does not create unnecessary burdens. Leveraging technology, outsourcing certain tasks, and maintaining organized processes can help maintain efficiency as your portfolio expands.

Risk management becomes even more critical as you scale. While leverage and growth create opportunities, they also increase exposure to potential risks. Maintaining reserves, diversifying income streams, and avoiding over-concentration in a single asset or market are essential strategies for preserving stability. A scalable system must be resilient, capable of withstanding market fluctuations and unexpected challenges.

Another advanced concept in scaling is sequencing deals strategically. Rather than executing transactions randomly, successful borrowers plan the order and timing of their refinances and investments. For example, refinancing a primary residence may provide better terms and higher LTV, which can then be used to fund investment property acquisitions. As those properties generate income, they strengthen the borrower's profile for future transactions. This strategic sequencing maximizes efficiency and accelerates growth.

Credit profile management continues to play a role in scalability. As your portfolio grows, maintaining strong credit becomes increasingly important for accessing favorable loan terms. This includes managing credit utilization, maintaining on-time payments, and periodically reviewing credit reports for accuracy. A strong credit profile enhances your ability to scale efficiently and reduces the cost of borrowing.

Liquidity remains a cornerstone of any scalable system. While it is important to deploy capital effectively, maintaining sufficient reserves ensures that you can continue operating and investing without interruption. Liquidity provides flexibility, allowing you to respond to opportunities and challenges without relying on high-cost debt or forced asset sales. A well-balanced system includes both active investments and accessible reserves. Another important factor is adaptability. Markets change, interest rates fluctuate, and opportunities evolve. A scalable system must be flexible enough to adjust to these changes. This may involve shifting strategies, exploring new markets, or modifying investment criteria. Borrowers who remain adaptable are better positioned to sustain growth over the long term.

Long-term vision ties all of these elements together. Scaling is not about rapid expansion at any cost—it is about building a sustainable, efficient, and profitable system that aligns with your financial goals. Whether your objective is to generate passive income, achieve financial independence, or create generational wealth, every decision should support that vision. This requires discipline, planning, and a commitment to continuous improvement.

Education and continuous learning are also essential. As you gain experience, you will encounter new challenges and opportunities. Staying informed about market trends, lending guidelines, and investment strategies allows you to refine your approach and maintain a competitive edge. The most successful borrowers are those who treat their financial journey as an ongoing process of learning and growth.

Ultimately, building a repeatable system for bank statement refinancing is about creating momentum. Each successful transaction builds on the last, creating a compounding effect that accelerates wealth creation. By focusing on consistency, efficiency, and strategic planning, you can transform individual deals into a cohesive system that supports long-term success.

Real-Life Math Example: Scaling a Portfolio Through a Repeatable Refinancing System

Now, for the next example let's talk about a borrower named Anthony, a self-employed consultant who begins with a primary residence valued at $700,000 and a mortgage balance of $350,000. His business generates consistent deposits of $25,000 per month, allowing him to qualify for a bank statement refinance. Anthony decides to implement a repeatable system to grow his real estate portfolio over time.

In the first cycle, Anthony refinances his primary residence at 75% LTV, resulting in a new loan of $525,000. After paying off his existing mortgage, he accesses $175,000 in equity, receiving approximately $160,000 after closing costs. He uses $120,000 as down payments on two investment properties, each priced at $300,000, and sets aside $40,000 as reserves.

Each property generates $2,200 per month in rental income,

with mortgage payments of $1,600, resulting in $600 in net cash flow per property. Combined, these properties generate $1,200 per month in net income. Anthony's new mortgage payment increases by $1,500, but the rental income offsets most of this increase, resulting in a manageable net change.

Over the next two years, Anthony's properties appreciate by an average of 5% annually. The two investment properties increase in value to approximately $330,000 each, while his primary residence increases to $770,000. His rental income also increases slightly due to market adjustments, improving overall cash flow.

In the second cycle, Anthony refinances one of his investment properties, now valued at $330,000, at 70% LTV. This results in a new loan of $231,000. After paying off the existing mortgage of $240,000, he does not extract cash but improves his loan terms and positions the property for future refinancing. He then refinances his primary residence again, now valued at $770,000, accessing additional equity.

This second refinance provides approximately $150,000 in new capital, which Anthony uses to acquire another investment property. This property generates $2,400 per month in rental income with a mortgage payment of $1,800, resulting in $600 in net cash flow. At this point, Anthony's portfolio includes three investment properties generating a combined net income of $1,800 per month.

In the third cycle, Anthony continues to repeat the process. As his portfolio grows and his income increases, he qualifies for larger loans and accesses more capital. After five years, his portfolio includes five investment properties and a primary residence, with a total value exceeding $2.5 million. His combined rental income generates over $4,000 per month in net cash flow.

Throughout this process, Anthony maintains reserves, manages risk, and continuously monitors performance. His system allows him to scale efficiently while maintaining stability. The initial refinance of his primary residence becomes the foundation for a series of transactions that build wealth over time.

This example demonstrates how a repeatable system can transform a single refinance into a scalable strategy for long-term growth. By following a structured process and maintaining discipline, borrowers can create a cycle of equity, investment, and income that continues to expand over time.

Chapter 12

Mastering the Complete System—From First Refinance to Financial Independence

At this final stage, everything comes together. Bank statement refinancing is no longer just a strategy—it becomes a complete financial system designed to create, expand, protect, and eventually stabilize wealth. From understanding deposits and structuring loans to managing risk, scaling portfolios, and planning exits, you now have the tools to operate at a high level. This chapter is about integrating all of these components into a unified approach that leads to financial independence, control, and long-term security.

Financial independence is not defined by a specific number—it is defined by control. It is the point at which your income from assets, investments, and business activities is sufficient to cover your expenses, allowing you to make decisions based on opportunity rather than necessity. Bank statement refinancing plays a critical role in reaching this point because it allows you to unlock capital, build income streams, and accelerate growth without being limited by traditional income documentation. The journey begins with the first refinance, but it does not end there. Each refinance should be viewed as a stepping stone within a larger system. The goal is not simply to access equity, but to deploy that equity in a way that creates additional income and opportunities. This creates a compounding effect, where each step builds on the previous one. Over time, this compounding becomes the engine of wealth creation.

A key principle in mastering this system is alignment. Every decision—whether it involves refinancing, investing, or allocating capital—must align with your long-term goals. This requires clarity about what you want to achieve. Are you focused on maximizing cash flow, building long-term appreciation, reducing risk, or creating a balanced portfolio? The answer will guide your strategy and influence how you structure your loans and investments.

Cash flow is the lifeblood of financial independence. While equity and appreciation contribute to net worth, consistent income provides stability and flexibility. A well-designed system prioritizes income-generating assets that produce reliable cash flow. This income can be used to cover living expenses, reinvest in new opportunities, or pay down debt. Over time, as cash flow increases, dependence on active income decreases, moving you closer to financial independence. Debt management remains a central component of the system. While leverage is essential for growth, it must be managed carefully to ensure sustainability. This involves balancing loan amounts, interest rates, and payment structures with income and reserves. As your financial position strengthens, you may choose to reduce leverage, refinance into better terms, or pay down debt to increase net income. The goal is to transition from growth-focused leverage to stability-focused efficiency over time.

Another important aspect is adaptability. Markets change, opportunities evolve, and personal circumstances shift. A successful system must be flexible enough to adjust to these changes. This might involve shifting from aggressive growth to conservative management, exploring new investment opportunities, or restructuring existing assets. The ability to adapt ensures that your system remains effective regardless of external conditions.

Liquidity continues to play a vital role even at advanced stages. While much of your capital may be invested, maintaining accessible reserves ensures that you can respond to opportunities and challenges without disruption. Liquidity provides confidence and control, allowing you to operate from a position of strength.

Portfolio diversification enhances both stability and growth. By spreading investments across different property types, markets, and income sources, you reduce exposure to any single risk. This creates a more resilient system that can withstand fluctuations and continue generating income. Diversification also opens the door to new opportunities, expanding your potential for growth.

Tax efficiency becomes increasingly important as your portfolio grows. Understanding how to structure your investments and refinancing strategies in a tax-efficient manner can significantly impact your net returns. This includes leveraging deductions, depreciation, and strategic timing of transactions. Working with knowledgeable professionals ensures that your system is optimized for both performance and compliance.

Legacy planning is the final layer of the system. For many individuals, the ultimate goal is not just personal financial independence, but the creation of lasting wealth that can benefit future generations. This involves structuring assets, planning for succession, and ensuring that your financial system can continue operating beyond your direct involvement. Bank statement refinancing can support this by providing the flexibility needed to adapt and grow over time.

The psychological aspect of financial independence should not be overlooked. Achieving control over your finances changes how you think, make decisions, and approach opportunities. Confidence replaces uncertainty, and strategy replaces reaction. This mindset shift is one of the most valuable outcomes of mastering this system.

As you integrate all of these elements, you will begin to see your financial life as a cohesive system rather than a series of isolated decisions. Each refinance, each investment, and each adjustment becomes part of a larger framework designed to support your goals. This level of integration is what separates those who achieve financial independence from those who remain dependent on a single income source.

Ultimately, mastering bank statement refinancing is about more than loans and numbers—it is about creating a life of freedom, flexibility, and opportunity. By applying the principles outlined in this book, you can build a system that not only generates wealth but also sustains and protects it over time.

Real-Life Math Example: From First Refinance to Financial Independence

Let's talk about a borrower named Sofia, a self-employed entrepreneur who begins her journey with a primary residence valued at $600,000 and a mortgage balance of $300,000. Her business generates consistent deposits of $20,000 per month, allowing her to qualify for a bank statement refinance. Sofia's goal is to build a system that leads to financial independence within 7 to 10 years.

In her first refinance, Sofia accesses $150,000 in equity after costs. She uses $100,000 as down payments on two investment properties priced at $250,000 each and sets aside $50,000 as reserves. Each property generates $1,800 per month in rental income with mortgage payments of $1,300, resulting in $500 in net cash flow per property. Combined, these properties generate $1,000 per month in net income.

Over the next two years, Sofia's properties appreciate and her rental income increases to $2,000 per property, raising her net cash flow to $1,400 per month. Her primary residence also appreciates to $660,000, increasing her available equity. She refinances again, accessing an additional $120,000, which she uses to acquire another investment property generating $600 in net monthly income.

At this stage, Sofia's portfolio includes three investment properties generating $2,000 per month in net cash flow. Her business continues to grow, increasing her monthly deposits to

$25,000. She maintains reserves and carefully manages her debt, ensuring that her system remains stable.

Over the next three years, Sofia repeats the process. She refinances strategically, acquires additional properties, and increases rental income. By year seven, her portfolio includes six investment properties, each generating an average of $600 in net monthly income, for a total of $3,600 per month. Her primary residence is largely paid down, reducing her housing costs.

Sofia's total monthly cash flow from rental properties reaches $4,500, which covers her living expenses. At this point, she achieves financial independence, as her passive income is sufficient to support her lifestyle. She continues to refine her system, reducing leverage and increasing efficiency.

Over time, Sofia may choose to sell certain properties, refinance into lower-rate loans, or reinvest in new opportunities. Her system remains flexible, allowing her to adapt to changing conditions while maintaining financial independence.

This example illustrates how bank statement refinancing can be used as a foundation for a complete financial system. By starting with a single refinance and applying consistent strategy, discipline, and planning, borrowers can build a pathway to financial independence and long-term success.

Chapter 13

Creating Your Personal Blueprint—From Knowledge to Execution

Reaching this point means you now understand the full system—how to qualify, how to structure, how to refinance, how to scale, and how to manage risk. But knowledge alone does not create results. Execution does. The difference between those who achieve financial independence and those who remain stuck is not access to information—it is the ability to take that information and turn it into a clear, actionable, repeatable blueprint. This chapter is about building that blueprint. It is about taking everything you have learned and converting it into a personalized system that you can follow step by step.

A blueprint is not a generic plan. It is tailored to your income, your goals, your risk tolerance, and your timeline. It begins with defining your starting point. This includes your current property value, loan balance, monthly income based on bank statements, credit profile, and available reserves. Without clarity on where you are, it is impossible to determine where you are going. This initial assessment is the foundation of your blueprint. Once your starting point is clear, the next step is defining your target outcome. This may include a specific monthly passive income goal, a portfolio size, or a timeline for achieving financial independence. For example, you may decide that your goal is to generate $5,000 per month in net rental income within five years. This target provides direction and allows you to reverse-engineer the steps needed to achieve it.

The next phase is identifying your first move. For most borrowers, this is a bank statement cash-out refinance. The objective of this refinance is not just to access equity, but to create momentum. The funds obtained should be allocated strategically—typically a combination of investment, reserves, and possibly debt reduction. The key is to ensure that the capital is used in a way that generates additional income or strengthens your financial position.

From there, your blueprint should outline a repeatable cycle. This cycle includes building equity, refinancing, deploying capital, increasing income, and repeating the process. Each cycle should move you closer to your target outcome. The timing of each cycle will depend on factors such as property appreciation, income growth, and market conditions. Your blueprint should include estimated timelines, but also remain flexible to adapt to changes.

Income management is a critical component of execution. Since bank statement loans rely on deposits, maintaining consistent and well-documented income is essential. This may involve structuring your business finances to create predictable deposit patterns, separating accounts, and avoiding unnecessary fluctuations. Treating your income profile as a strategic asset ensures that you remain eligible for future refinances.

Another important element is deal criteria. Not every investment will contribute equally to your goals. Your blueprint should define clear criteria for evaluating opportunities. This might include minimum cash flow requirements, acceptable price ranges, target locations, and risk thresholds. By establishing these criteria in advance, you reduce the likelihood of making impulsive or suboptimal decisions.

Capital allocation is where strategy meets execution. Each time you access equity, you must decide how to distribute those funds. A balanced approach often includes allocating a portion to income-generating investments, a portion to reserves, and a portion to strengthening your financial position. This balance ensures that you are growing while also maintaining stability.

Tracking and accountability are essential for maintaining

momentum. Your blueprint should include a system for monitoring progress, including metrics such as cash flow, property values, loan balances, and overall net worth. Regularly reviewing these metrics allows you to identify areas for improvement and adjust your strategy as needed. Without tracking, it is easy to lose direction or overlook opportunities.

Risk management remains integrated into every step of the blueprint. This includes maintaining reserves, avoiding over-leverage, and planning for different scenarios. Your blueprint should account for both growth and protection, ensuring that your system is resilient as it scales.

Another key component is building a support network. This includes professionals such as mortgage brokers, CPAs, real estate agents, and property managers who understand your strategy and can help you execute it effectively. Having the right team in place can significantly improve efficiency and outcomes.

Mindset and discipline are the final pieces of the blueprint. Execution requires consistency, patience, and a willingness to follow the plan even when results are not immediate. There will be challenges, market changes, and unexpected obstacles. Staying focused on your long-term goals and maintaining discipline is what allows the blueprint to work over time.

Your blueprint is not static—it evolves as your situation changes. As your income grows, your portfolio expands, and your goals shift, your blueprint should be updated to reflect these changes. This adaptability ensures that your system remains aligned with your objectives.

Ultimately, creating your personal blueprint is about taking control. It is about moving from reactive decisions to proactive strategy. It is about building a system that you understand, trust, and can execute with confidence. This is where knowledge becomes action, and action becomes results.

Real-Life Math Example: Building and Executing a Personal Blueprint

For this example, we will review a borrower named Carlos, a self-employed consultant with a primary residence valued at $650,000 and a mortgage balance of $300,000. His bank statements show consistent monthly deposits of $22,000. Carlos sets a goal to achieve $5,000 per month in net rental income within six years.

In his first step, Carlos completes a bank statement cash-out refinance at 75% LTV, resulting in a new loan of $487,500. After paying off his existing mortgage, he accesses $187,500 in equity, receiving approximately $175,000 after closing costs. He allocates $120,000 as down payments on two investment properties priced at $300,000 each and sets aside $55,000 as reserves.

Each property generates $2,200 per month in rental income with mortgage payments of $1,600, resulting in $600 in net cash flow per property. Combined, these properties generate $1,200 per month in net income. Carlos tracks his progress and maintains consistent income deposits to prepare for future refinances.

After two years, his properties appreciate to $330,000 each, and rental income increases to $2,400 per property, raising net cash flow to $1,600 per month. His primary residence appreciates to $715,000, increasing his available equity. He completes a second refinance, accessing $140,000 in additional capital.

Carlos uses this capital to acquire two more properties, each generating $600 in net monthly income. At this stage, his total net rental income reaches $2,800 per month. He continues to maintain reserves and follows his blueprint, ensuring that each step aligns with his goal.

Over the next three years, Carlos repeats the process. He acquires additional properties, increases rental income, and optimizes his portfolio. By year six, he owns six investment properties, each generating an average of $850 in net monthly income, for a total of $5,100 per month.

At this point, Carlos achieves his goal of $5,000 per month in passive income. His blueprint has guided him from a single property to a diversified portfolio that supports his financial independence. He continues to refine his system, focusing on stability and long-term growth.

This example demonstrates how a clear and structured blueprint can turn knowledge into results. By defining goals, executing consistently, and adapting over time, borrowers can create a system that leads to financial independence and long-term success.

Chapter 14

The Ultimate Wealth Flywheel—Automating Growth, Income, and Freedom

At the highest level, everything you have learned converges into a single powerful concept: the wealth flywheel. A flywheel is a system that, once set in motion, continues to build momentum with less effort over time. In the context of bank statement refinancing and real estate investing, the flywheel represents a self-reinforcing cycle where equity, income, and opportunity continuously feed into one another. Instead of relying on constant effort or active income, you create a system that begins to operate with increasing efficiency, generating results that compound year after year.

The flywheel begins with a simple but powerful sequence: acquire or hold an asset, build equity, access that equity through refinancing, deploy capital into income-producing opportunities, increase cash flow, and repeat. Each step strengthens the next. As equity grows, your ability to refinance increases. As you refinance, your access to capital expands. As you deploy that capital into investments, your income grows. As your income grows, your ability to qualify for future loans improves. This cycle creates momentum, and over time, that momentum becomes the engine of wealth creation.

One of the defining characteristics of the flywheel is that it becomes easier to maintain as it grows. In the early stages, each refinance and investment requires significant effort and attention. However, as your portfolio expands and your income increases, each additional step becomes more efficient. Your experience improves, your processes become streamlined, and your access to opportunities expands. What once required effort begins to feel automatic.

Automation is a key element of this process. While the term "automation" often refers to technology, in this context it also includes systems, processes, and delegation. Property management can be outsourced, financial tracking can be systemized, and decision-making frameworks can be standardized. By reducing the amount of manual effort required, you free up time and energy to focus on higher-level strategy and growth.

Income diversification strengthens the flywheel by adding multiple sources of momentum. Rental income, business income, and other investments all contribute to your overall financial engine. When one source fluctuates, others can compensate, maintaining stability. This diversification not only reduces risk but also accelerates growth, as multiple streams of income contribute to your ability to reinvest and expand.

Another critical aspect of the flywheel is reinvestment discipline. The temptation to consume income rather than reinvest it can slow or even stop the momentum. Successful borrowers understand that the early and middle stages of the flywheel require a focus on growth. By reinvesting a significant portion of income into new opportunities, they accelerate the compounding effect. Over time, as the system matures, they can gradually shift toward enjoying the income while maintaining the core structure.

Efficiency becomes increasingly important as the flywheel grows. This includes optimizing loan structures, reducing costs, and improving returns on investment. For example, refinancing into better terms, consolidating properties, or upgrading assets can enhance overall performance. Each improvement adds to the momentum, making the system more effective and sustainable.

Leverage continues to play a role, but it evolves over time. In the early stages, leverage is used aggressively to build the flywheel. As the system matures, the focus shifts toward optimizing and stabilizing leverage. This may involve paying down debt, refinancing into lower rates, or maintaining conservative loan-to-value ratios. The goal is to preserve the momentum while reducing risk.

Another advanced concept is velocity of capital. This refers to how quickly capital is deployed and redeployed within the system. Faster capital movement leads to faster growth, as each dollar is used more efficiently. This requires careful planning, quick decision-making, and a clear understanding of opportunities. Bank statement refinancing supports this by providing flexible access to capital when needed.

Time becomes one of the most powerful factors in the flywheel. The longer the system operates, the more pronounced the compounding effect becomes. Appreciation, income growth, and reinvestment all contribute to exponential results over time. This is why consistency and patience are essential. The flywheel does not produce maximum results immediately, but over time, it can create significant wealth.

Another important element is adaptability. While the flywheel provides structure, it must remain flexible to adjust to changing conditions. Market shifts, interest rate changes, and new opportunities all require adjustments to the system. Borrowers who remain adaptable can maintain momentum even in changing environments. The psychological shift that occurs during this process is profound. Instead of chasing income, you begin to manage a system that produces it. Decision-making becomes more strategic, and financial stress is replaced with confidence. This shift is one of the most valuable outcomes of building the flywheel.

Ultimately, the goal of the wealth flywheel is not just growth, but freedom. Financial freedom comes from having a system that generates sufficient income to support your lifestyle while continuing to grow. It allows you to make choices based on preference rather than necessity, creating a level of control that is difficult to achieve through traditional income alone.

By the time you reach this stage, bank statement refinancing is no longer just a tool—it is part of a larger system that supports your entire financial life. It provides the flexibility, access, and scalability needed to build and sustain the flywheel. When combined with disciplined execution and strategic thinking, it becomes a powerful engine for long-term success.

Real-Life Math Example: Building and Accelerating the Wealth Flywheel

For this example, we will go over a borrower named Elena, a self-employed entrepreneur who begins with a primary residence valued at $700,000 and a mortgage balance of $350,000. Her bank statements show consistent monthly deposits of $24,000. Elena's goal is to build a wealth flywheel that generates at least $8,000 per month in passive income within eight years.

In the first stage, Elena completes a bank statement cash-out refinance at 75% LTV, resulting in a new loan of $525,000. After paying off her existing mortgage, she accesses $175,000 in equity, receiving approximately $160,000 after closing costs. She allocates $120,000 as down payments on two investment properties priced at $300,000 each and sets aside $40,000 as reserves.

Each property generates $2,200 per month in rental income with mortgage payments of $1,600, resulting in $600 in net cash flow per property. Combined, these properties generate $1,200 per month in net income. This marks the beginning of her flywheel.

Over the next two years, Elena reinvests her rental income and business profits. Her properties appreciate to $330,000 each, and rental income increases to $2,400 per property, raising net cash flow to $1,600 per month. She refinances again, accessing an additional $150,000, which she uses to acquire two more properties.

At this stage, Elena owns four investment properties generating a combined net income of $2,400 per month. Her flywheel begins to accelerate as each property contributes to her income and equity growth.

In the third stage, Elena focuses on efficiency and optimization. She improves property management, reduces expenses, and increases rental income through strategic upgrades. Her average net cash flow per property increases to $800 per month. With four properties, this results in $3,200 per month in passive income.

She then executes another refinance cycle, using increased equity and income to acquire two additional properties. These properties generate similar returns, bringing her total to six properties with $4,800 per month in net income.

By year six, Elena's flywheel is operating at full momentum. Her portfolio continues to appreciate, and her income grows steadily. She refines her strategy, balancing growth with stability, and begins to reduce leverage on certain properties.

By year eight, Elena's portfolio includes eight properties, each generating an average of $1,000 in net monthly income, for a total of $8,000 per month. At this point, she achieves her goal of financial freedom. Her flywheel continues to operate, generating income and opportunities with minimal additional effort. This example demonstrates how the wealth flywheel can transform a single refinance into a dynamic, self-sustaining system. By consistently reinvesting, optimizing, and adapting, borrowers can create a cycle of growth that leads to long-term financial independence and freedom.

Chapter 15

Sustaining Wealth, Protecting Your Portfolio, and Living the Outcome

Reaching the point where your system is working—where income is flowing, assets are growing, and opportunities are abundant—is a powerful achievement. But the final stage of mastery is not just about building wealth; it is about sustaining it, protecting it, and ultimately living the outcome it was designed to create. Many borrowers focus intensely on growth but fail to fully transition into preservation and optimization. This chapter is about making that transition intentionally—ensuring that what you have built continues to serve you for decades to come.

Sustaining wealth begins with a shift in mindset. Early in the journey, the focus is on expansion: acquiring properties, increasing income, and maximizing leverage. As the system matures, the focus gradually shifts toward stability, efficiency, and control. This does not mean stopping growth entirely—it means becoming more selective, more strategic, and more focused on quality over quantity. Instead of asking "How can I grow faster?" the question becomes "How can I make what I have stronger, more efficient, and more resilient?" One of the most important strategies for sustaining wealth is optimizing your debt structure. Over time, you may choose to refinance into lower interest rates, shorter loan terms, or more favorable conditions as your financial profile improves. Reducing interest costs and improving loan efficiency can significantly increase your net cash flow. In some cases, paying down certain loans—particularly those with higher rates—can provide a guaranteed return equivalent to the interest saved.

Another key element is strengthening your cash flow foundation. While growth strategies often prioritize expansion, long-term sustainability requires consistent and reliable income. This may involve focusing on properties with stable rental demand, improving tenant quality, or upgrading assets to increase rental income. The goal is to ensure that your portfolio generates sufficient cash flow not only to cover expenses, but to provide a comfortable margin of safety.

Reserves remain critical even at advanced stages. While your portfolio may generate substantial income, maintaining accessible reserves ensures that you can handle unexpected expenses, vacancies, or market fluctuations without disruption. Many experienced investors maintain reserves equivalent to 6 to 12 months of expenses, or more, depending on their risk tolerance and portfolio size. This level of preparedness provides peace of mind and reinforces long-term stability. Portfolio pruning is another advanced strategy for sustaining wealth. Not every asset will continue to perform optimally over time. Some properties may underperform, require excessive management, or no longer align with your goals. Periodically reviewing your portfolio and identifying assets that may be better sold or repositioned allows you to maintain efficiency. The capital from these sales can be redeployed into higher-performing opportunities or used to reduce debt.

Tax efficiency becomes increasingly important as your portfolio grows. Strategic planning around depreciation, capital gains, and refinancing can significantly impact your net returns. For example, refinancing allows you to access equity without triggering a taxable event, while depreciation can offset rental income. Working with knowledgeable professionals ensures that your strategy is optimized from a tax perspective, preserving more of your wealth.

Another important aspect is asset protection. As your net worth increases, protecting your assets from potential risks becomes essential. This may involve structuring ownership through entities, maintaining appropriate insurance coverage, and implementing legal safeguards. Asset protection is not about avoiding risk entirely, but about managing it in a way that preserves your financial position. Lifestyle alignment is a defining feature of this stage. The purpose of building wealth is not just accumulation—it is to create the freedom to live on your own terms. This might include reducing work hours, pursuing personal interests, traveling, or spending more time with family. Your financial system should support your desired lifestyle, not restrict it. This requires a conscious decision to transition from growth-focused behavior to enjoyment and balance.

Another advanced concept is income layering. Even at this stage, you may choose to maintain multiple income streams, including rental income, business income, and other investments. This diversification enhances stability and provides additional flexibility. However, the emphasis shifts from maximizing income to optimizing and maintaining it.

Legacy planning becomes a central focus. For many individuals, sustaining wealth includes ensuring that it can be passed on effectively to future generations. This involves structuring assets, planning for succession, and creating systems that can continue operating beyond your direct involvement. Clear documentation, education, and communication are key components of this process.

Emotional discipline remains essential throughout. Markets will continue to fluctuate, and opportunities will continue to arise. The ability to remain grounded, avoid impulsive decisions, and stay aligned with your long-term goals ensures that your system remains effective. This discipline is what allows wealth to be sustained rather than diminished.

Another important consideration is knowing when enough is enough. The drive to grow can be powerful, but it must be balanced with the recognition of when your goals have been achieved. At that point, the focus can shift toward preservation, enjoyment, and legacy. This transition is not always easy, but it is essential for fully realizing the benefits of your efforts.

Ultimately, sustaining wealth is about creating a system that continues to work for you without constant intervention. It is about building resilience, optimizing performance, and aligning your financial life with your personal values. Bank statement refinancing, which played a critical role in building your system, now becomes a tool for maintaining and refining it.

Real-Life Math Example: Transitioning from Growth to Stability and Financial Freedom

Consider a borrower named Victor, a self-employed entrepreneur who has spent the past decade building a real estate portfolio using bank statement refinancing strategies. Victor owns a primary residence valued at $900,000 with a mortgage balance of $400,000, along with eight investment properties with a combined value of $3.2 million and total debt of $2 million. His portfolio generates $12,000 per month in net rental income.

Victor's monthly living expenses are $6,000, meaning his rental income alone more than covers his lifestyle. At this stage, Victor shifts his focus from aggressive growth to sustainability and optimization.

Victor begins by analyzing his debt structure. Several of his properties have interest rates above 7%, while current market conditions allow for refinancing at 6%. He refinances three of these properties, reducing his combined monthly payments by $900. This increases his net cash flow from $12,000 to $12,900 per month.

Next, Victor evaluates his portfolio and identifies two properties that require significant management and generate lower returns. He decides to sell these properties, netting $300,000 after expenses. He uses $200,000 to pay down debt on his primary residence, reducing his mortgage balance to $200,000 and lowering his monthly payment by $1,200. The remaining $100,000 is added to his reserves.

Victor now has reserves of $200,000, providing more than two years of coverage for his living expenses. His adjusted portfolio generates $10,500 per month in net rental income after the sale of the two properties. Combined with his reduced expenses, his financial position remains strong and stable. Victor also invests $50,000 into upgrading one of his remaining properties, increasing its rental income by $500 per month. This brings his total net rental income to $11,000 per month. His monthly expenses, now reduced to $4,800 due to lower debt payments, are easily covered by his income.

Over time, Victor continues to optimize his portfolio, focusing on efficiency and stability. He maintains strong reserves, monitors performance, and avoids unnecessary risk. His financial system now supports his desired lifestyle, allowing him to reduce his active work and focus on personal goals.

Victor's journey illustrates the transition from growth to sustainability. By refinancing strategically, managing debt, optimizing his portfolio, and aligning his system with his lifestyle, he creates a stable and resilient financial structure. His wealth is no longer just growing—it is supporting a life of freedom and control.

This final example demonstrates the ultimate outcome of mastering bank statement refinancing and cash-out strategies. It is not just about building wealth—it is about sustaining it, protecting it, and living the life it was meant to create.

Final Thoughts

From Strategy to Legacy—Your Financial Evolution

As you reach the end of this journey, it is important to pause and recognize what you have truly built. This is not just a collection of strategies, loan programs, or investment techniques. What you now understand is a complete financial framework—a system that allows you to take control of your income, your assets, and your future. Bank statement mortgage loans were the entry point, but the real outcome is far greater. You now possess the ability to think differently, act strategically, and create opportunities where others see limitations.

Throughout this journey, one principle has remained constant: flexibility creates opportunity. Traditional financial systems often limit borrowers based on rigid definitions of income and risk. Bank statement financing breaks through those limitations by recognizing real-world cash flow and entrepreneurial income. But beyond that, it teaches a deeper lesson—that financial success is not about fitting into a system, but about understanding how the system works and using it to your advantage. This shift in perspective is one of the most valuable outcomes of everything you have learned.

You have seen how equity, when left unused, remains dormant, but when accessed and deployed strategically, becomes a powerful engine for growth. You have learned how to transform debt from a burden into a tool, how to convert expenses into investments, and how to build income streams that operate independently of your time. These are not just tactics—they are transformations in how you approach money, risk, and opportunity.

At the beginning, the process may have seemed complex. Understanding deposits, expense ratios, loan-to-value limits, and lender guidelines requires attention and discipline. But over time, these elements become familiar, and eventually, they become second nature. What once felt like a complicated system becomes a set of tools that you can use with confidence. This progression—from uncertainty to mastery—is what allows you to move forward with clarity and purpose.

One of the most important lessons is that progress is built through consistency. There is no single transaction that creates lasting wealth. It is the repetition of smart decisions—refinancing at the right time, investing strategically, managing risk, and maintaining discipline—that produces results. Each step may seem incremental, but together, they create a compounding effect that becomes increasingly powerful over time. This is how ordinary actions, when executed consistently, lead to extraordinary outcomes. You have also learned that growth and protection must work together. It is easy to focus on expansion—acquiring more properties, increasing income, and maximizing leverage. But true success requires balance. Maintaining reserves, managing risk, and protecting your assets ensures that your system remains stable even as it grows. This balance is what allows you to sustain wealth rather than simply create it.

Another key realization is that your financial journey is uniquely yours. The strategies outlined in this book provide a framework, but the way you apply them will depend on your goals, your resources, and your vision. There is no single path to success, but there are principles that apply to every path. By understanding these principles, you can adapt and evolve your strategy as your circumstances change.

The concept of the wealth flywheel represents the culmination of everything you have learned. It is the point where your system begins to operate with momentum, where each step reinforces the next, and where growth becomes more efficient over time. Reaching this stage requires effort and discipline, but once achieved, it creates a level of financial control that is difficult to replicate through traditional means. It is not about working harder—it is about building a system that works for you. As your system matures, your focus naturally shifts. What begins as a pursuit of growth evolves into a pursuit of freedom. Financial independence is not just about numbers—it is about having the ability to choose how you spend your time, where you invest your energy, and what opportunities you pursue. It is about creating a life that aligns with your values and priorities. The strategies you have learned are tools to help you reach that point, but the outcome is much broader than financial success alone.

Legacy is the final layer of this journey. The wealth you build has the potential to extend beyond your own lifetime, creating opportunities for others and leaving a lasting impact. This requires intentional planning, clear structure, and a commitment to preserving what you have created. It also involves sharing knowledge and guiding others, ensuring that the system you have built can continue to operate and grow.

There will be challenges along the way. Markets will change, opportunities will vary, and unexpected events will occur. But the strength of your system lies in its adaptability. By staying informed, maintaining discipline, and continuously refining your approach, you can navigate these challenges and continue moving forward. The ability to adapt is what separates those who succeed in the long term from those who struggle to maintain progress.

Confidence is one of the most powerful outcomes of this process. As you gain experience and see results, your confidence in your ability to make decisions and execute strategies grows. This confidence allows you to act decisively, take calculated risks, and pursue opportunities with clarity. It transforms uncertainty into opportunity and hesitation into action.

It is also important to remember that success is not defined solely by financial metrics. While income, equity, and net worth are important, they are means to an end. The ultimate goal is to create a life that is fulfilling, balanced, and aligned with your values. This includes time with family, personal growth, health, and experiences that bring meaning to your life. Your financial system should support these goals, not overshadow them.

As you move forward, take time to reflect on your progress and adjust your strategy as needed. Regular evaluation ensures that you remain aligned with your goals and continue to optimize your system. This process of reflection and adjustment is what keeps your strategy effective over time.

The journey does not end here—it evolves. Each new opportunity, each decision, and each refinement adds to your experience and strengthens your system. The knowledge you have gained is not static; it is a foundation that you will continue to build upon.

You now have the tools, the understanding, and the framework to take control of your financial future. The next step is action. By applying what you have learned, maintaining discipline, and staying focused on your goals, you can create a system that supports growth, stability, and freedom.

This is not just about mortgages. This is about transformation.

How to Get a Personalized Bank Statement Mortgage Review

If you found this book helpful, you may want to see how these strategies apply to your specific financial situation.

Bank statement mortgage lending is highly customized—your deposits, income patterns, expense ratios, credit profile, property type, and long-term goals all play a role in determining what you qualify for and how your loan should be structured.

Every borrower's situation is different. The way your income flows through your accounts, how your business operates, your credit history, the property you are purchasing or refinancing, and current lender guidelines all impact your options. The strategies and examples in this book are designed to teach you how bank statement mortgage loans work—but your actual qualifying income, loan amount, and loan structure can only be determined by analyzing your real financial profile.

If you would like a no-obligation Bank Statement Mortgage review, you can request one here:

Email: info@FinibiMortgage.com

A licensed mortgage broker will review your bank statements, income structure, credit profile, and goals, and explain what bank statement mortgage options may be available to you—including:

• 12-month and 24-month bank statement programs• Personal vs business bank statement qualification• Primary residence and investment property financing• Cash-out refinance and equity access strategies• Advanced structuring to maximize qualifying income

No cost. No pressure. No obligation.

Sincerely,

Joseph G. Correa

Finibi Mortgage Inc.

Licensed Mortgage Broker

About the Author

Joseph G. Correa is a licensed mortgage broker and the founder of Finibi Mortgage, a Florida-based brokerage specializing in bank statement mortgage loans, non-QM lending, and strategic real estate financing solutions for self-employed borrowers, entrepreneurs, and investors.

With more than two decades of experience in mortgage lending, underwriting, and deal structuring, Joseph has helped thousands of clients qualify for real estate using alternative income documentation, unlocking opportunities that traditional lending often restricts.

Unlike traditional loan officers who rely strictly on tax returns and W-2 income, Joseph's approach focuses on real cash flow, income structuring, and financial strategy. He believes that borrowers should not be limited by how income is reported on paper, but instead empowered by how income is actually earned and managed.

Joseph is widely recognized for his expertise in:

• Bank statement mortgage loans• Self-employed borrower financing• Non-QM and alternative income lending• Investment property and portfolio financing• Cash-out refinance and equity strategies• Advanced mortgage loan structuring

Through his education platform, Finibi Academy, Joseph has trained tens of thousands of students worldwide in mortgage strategy, real estate investing, credit optimization, and financial independence.

He created the **Bank Statement Mortgage Loan Mastery Series** to provide a clear, step-by-step roadmap for borrowers and professionals who want to qualify for real estate without relying on traditional income documentation.

His mission is simple: To help people use their real income—not just their tax returns—to qualify, invest, and build long-term wealth.

When he is not structuring loans or writing, Joseph works with clients across the United States to design customized mortgage strategies that align with their financial goals, income structure, and long-term investment plans.

The Bank Statement Mortgage Loan Mastery Series Roadmap

The Complete Guide to Qualifying for Real Estate Using Bank Statements Instead of Tax Returns

The purpose of the **Bank Statement Mortgage Loan Mastery Series** is to give borrowers, investors, and mortgage professionals the exact strategies used by lenders and underwriters—translated into simple, practical steps you can apply in real life.

This series takes you from beginner to advanced mastery of how to qualify, structure, and scale real estate financing using bank statements instead of traditional income.

Each book builds on the last. You are not just learning how to get approved—you are learning how to control your approvals.

Book 1 — Bank Statement Mortgage Loan Fundamentals

Learn how bank statement loans work, how income is calculated, and why tax returns are no longer required for many borrowers.

Book 2 — Personal Bank Statement Mortgage Loans

Learn how to qualify using personal accounts, structure

deposits, and maximize usable income.

Book 3 — Business Bank Statement Mortgage Loans

Understand how lenders analyze business revenue, apply expense ratios, and use P&Ls.

Book 4 — Bank Statement Loans for Self-Employed Borrowers

Master how entrepreneurs qualify and structure income for approval.

Book 5 — Bank Statement Loans for Primary Residences

Learn how to buy or refinance your home using bank statement income.

Book 6 — Bank Statement Loans for Investment Properties

Discover how to scale rental portfolios using bank statement + DSCR strategies.

Book 7 — Jumbo Bank Statement Mortgage Loans

Learn how to finance high-value properties with advanced requirements and structuring.

Book 8 — Bank Statement Loan Refinancing & Cash-Out Strategies

Unlock equity, reduce payments, and reinvest capital using bank statement refinancing.

Book 9 — Bank Statement Loans with Credit Challenges

Learn how to qualify even with lower credit using compensating factors and strategy.

Book 10 — Advanced Bank Statement Mortgage Loan Structuring

Engineer approvals using deposits, expense ratios, and lender guidelines.

This series is designed to move you from understanding → execution → mastery.

By the end, you will not just know how to qualify—you will know how to structure deals like a professional.

Educational & Financial Disclaimer

The **Bank Statement Mortgage Loan Mastery Series** is intended for educational and informational purposes only.

This content is designed to help readers understand bank statement mortgage lending, real estate financing strategies, and income structuring concepts. It is not financial, legal, tax, or investment advice.

Joseph G. Correa and Live Stronger Faster are not acting as your personal financial advisor, attorney, accountant, or mortgage professional through this publication.

Mortgage guidelines, underwriting standards, interest rates, and loan programs vary by lender and may change at any time without notice.

All examples in this series are for illustration purposes only and do not guarantee approval or results.

Always consult with licensed professionals before making financial decisions.

Risk Disclosure

Bank statement mortgage lending and real estate investing involve risk.

Income fluctuations, interest rate changes, market conditions, and lender guidelines can all impact loan approval and financial outcomes.

Borrowing against real estate or using leverage increases both potential returns and risks.

Failure to repay a loan may result in foreclosure and loss of property.

Cash flow, rental income, and appreciation are not guaranteed.

All strategies in this series are educational and must be evaluated based on your individual financial situation.

You are solely responsible for your financial decisions.

www.ingramcontent.com/pod-product-compliance
Ingram Content Group UK Ltd.
Pitfield, Milton Keynes, MK11 3LW, UK
UKHW020159290926
15471UKWH00005B/954

9 798295 813757